Living Out Loud

Design Your Life of Unlimited Possibilities

By Angela Wilson

Copyright 2022 by Angela Wilson
Living Out Loud – Design Your Life of Unlimited Possibilities

All rights reserved. Printed in the United States of America. No part of this book may be used or reproduced in any written form or by electronic or mechanical means, including information storage and retrieval systems, without written permission from the author, except for the use of brief quotations in a book review.

First published in the USA in 2022 by Angela Wilson

Note: The author is Canadian, so Canadian spelling is used in this book.

Paperback ISBN: 978-1-958405-41-3
eBook ISBN: 978-1-958405-40-6
Hardcover ISBN: 978-1-958405-42-0

Publisher: Spotlight Publishing House™ in Goodyear, AZ
https://SpotlightPublishingHouse.com

Editor: Susan Crossman – Crossman Communications
Book Cover: Cathy Dickinson Artist
Interior Design: Marigold2k

Living Out Loud

Design Your Life of Unlimited Possibilities

By Angela Wilson

Goodyear, Arizona

Contents

Endorsements...vii
Introduction..1
Living with Fraud Complex 5
Judgement: A Shadow Game 15
Losing Your Voice..25
The Protective Layers We Wrap Around Us...................37
Feelings of Low Self-Esteem and Low Self-Worth 45
Proving/Mattering is not Your Job 55
Inner Chatter is Debilitating! 65
Emotions Guide Us..75
Living in the Shadow of Shame 83
Hiding In Plain Sight 91
Living in the Shadows 99
Wanting to Fit In 109
Surviving Life is not Living 117
Intentional Dreaming..125
Choices. We Have Them! 131
Navigating to Be Seen 139
Life as a Double Agent 149
Being Alone...157
Being the Authentic You..163
Bibliography..173
About the Author 175

Advanced Praise

Angela Wilson has provided a great space to create a positive and welcoming relationship with money. I am much more confident and excited to live my life knowing that I now have the tools and knowledge to control my dreams!"
– **Rachel Becker**

Working with Angela has transformed my relationship to my personal finances as well as my beliefs surrounding money and abundance. Angela consistently encourages me to dream bigger and more creatively; when I do, she is prepared with multiple ways that my present or future financial situation can help accomplish my goals.

Every session with Angela has left me more empowered and confident in making informed and heart-centered decisions about my future. I am deeply grateful for the wisdom she has imparted to me, guiding me to deeply honor and invest in myself and my dreams.

I cannot imagine a better combination of intelligence/left-brain competence and genuine compassion and encouragement than that which Angela naturally brings to her financial coaching. I'd recommend her again and again!
– **Charlette Jones**

Angela's journey is a multi-layered story of bullying and low self-esteem. Step by step Angela shows us that what comes "after" counts way more than what went "before". Proof that the possibilities are endless when you believe in yourself. Now each day for her is a step forward. Angela's story is a must read for anyone who has suffered with these issues.
— **Kenza Warburton**

When I attended Angela Wilson's workshop, I thought it would just be a refresher on information I already knew; I left the program with a greater understanding of my attitudes toward money, and with very new ideas around making it work for me. I am much more motivated, and I'm confident that, not only can I meet my current goals, I can surpass them!

Then I read Angela's book.

I think that anyone who reads this book will connect with the content in some way - we all have that inner chatter, telling us that we can't do things. The voice is especially strong in girls, because not only is it parents, teachers, and friends; it's also books, tv, movies and magazines! I LOVED it!
— **Tania McClean**

Introduction

The evening had started off like many other dinners out with friends, so I was unprepared for the twist it ended up taking. As often happened, my then-partner and our friends began challenging each other with word games, something I wasn't very good at and definitely did not enjoy. I sat listening quietly and waited for the games to end. But that night the competition seemed to intensify.

Words and conversations flew across the table, and at first, I hoped no one would notice my lack of participation. And then the thought struck me: what would happen if I said nothing at all? And so, for the rest of that whole evening, I only spoke when I was directly addressed. And then I would go silent again. No one, not even my then-partner, realized what I was doing. Why was I even there? Clearly, I didn't matter if I could sit in silence for an entire evening and no one even noticed. My head filled with thoughts of how I didn't measure up, how I didn't matter, how I was worth-less. Later, as I drifted off to sleep, exhausted from trying to keep my composure, my heart whispered softly to me: *"There has to be more to life than this."*

This wasn't just a passing thought. It became the dominant theme of my life. In those days I often said—okay, mostly in my head—"*Isn't there more to* me *than this?*" And beyond that, I would think, "*There must be something creative inside me!*" If these thoughts—or something similar—have ever crossed your mind, please keep reading.

My sincere hope is that the words in this book will connect with everyone who can take them in. I say it that way because words have played such a big part in my life. Some words make us feel bad because of the way we internalized them following a perceptively negative experience. Well, that's the way it was for me, and I hope as my words spill out on to the page in front of you, you can relax, and know you are not alone.

I felt alone inside my head and inside my experience for a long time and it had a profound impact on my journey—my life. It is one of the reasons I decided to start a new company—Angela Unlimited—and to write this book. You see, feeling alone, unliked, and unloved created a place of fear for me. Actually, these thoughts paralyzed me, and they almost led to the end of my journey, my life. But for now, my primary intention is to intrigue you, invite you to laugh, and perhaps to shed a few tears…but most importantly I hope my story will assist you to start to sense the immense light within you. We are all unique individuals on our own unique journeys. But being unique does not mean having to be alone, to do things in solitude, or to conquer everything as a solo pilot navigating the globe. What it does invite you to do is to be brave enough to listen to your heart and your inner knowing. You know—that gut instinct, the part of you that *just knows things* and guides you to act. It means, going on the incredible journey of life, and opening yourself up to be seen by the world for the magnificence within you – what I call your inner magnificence.

We all have a story, and mine rolls from shadows to light and swings from unlimited to limited and back to unlimited again. Does that sound familiar in your life? Then I invite you to come on the adventure of discovering some of the most essential aspects of rediscovering and recreating the life you are meant to live. I was told and shown over and over again that I did not deserve the life I wanted. Over time I began to see a different truth and gradually released my hold on the stories I'd been hearing, and then believing for much of my life, the stories that had kept me quiet for decades. Seeing a different truth is available to you too, if you have the curiosity and courage to see what other possibilities there are.

I've specifically written this book to focus on issues that I and my clients have all struggled with and resolved and I know from experience that those issues don't always crop up in a nice linear fashion. I invite you to read this book according to how you're feeling: if you want to start at the beginning and read until the end, that's great, but it's probably equally helpful to just pick a chapter from the Table of Contents that resonates with you and dive in there.

No matter where you are on your journey to get back to the path to the life you are meant to live, please keep searching. Because one day you will soar out the other side of whatever cloud is surrounding you and you will be able to fully shine your own magnificent light for all the world to see. It's possible. And I believe in you.

For my personal message
Scan the QR Code with your smart phone
Or go to: https://youtu.be/HEYYMob5Wps

Chapter One

Living with Fraud Complex

*It's hard to navigate through life hearing
the voice inside you screaming that you are a fraud.*
—Angela Wilson

I walked into the office with my shoulders back and my head held high: I was a calm, steely-eyed professional who had earned her place in this business and there was no way I was going to let anyone know that, despite the professional, competent-looking exterior I showed to the world, *inside* I was a white-hot mess. I was a designated accountant by day handling millions of dollars of other people's money. And I could barely balance my household bank accounts. My personal finances were a disaster.

Have you ever felt like a *fraud*?

A lot of people won't *admit* to feeling like a fraud, but I'm going to guess most of us—at one time or another—have felt like one. That's a pretty heavy word, so let's take a step back and I will explain what I mean. In my definition of the word, being a fraud is hiding the hot-mess side of you under the façade of having everything handled. In my case, the hot-mess part came about because I wanted approval badly enough to change my behaviour, my preferences, and even sometimes my values to the point where I didn't even know who I was anymore. I felt like that for a lot of years.

I often told others I was like two different people. I know some people thought that was impossible, and I let them go on believing what they wanted to believe because in my heart I knew what was really happening. I was the "work Angela" and the "home Angela."

You see, at work I was the consummate professional. As a designated accountant I felt there were certain expectations around how I should act and how I should carry myself. Don't let anyone in. Don't let anyone know you can be a goof. Don't let anyone see that you actually don't have everything handled. After all, the people you work for are entrusting you with their financial well-being. I always worked in the corporate world where I was involved with company funds rather than people's personal funds. Really, though, when we look at the finances of a company, we can see they truly are personal finances on some level because people get paid from those funds and the owners receive their personal income from them as well. It all comes back to personal finances eventually.

So, at work I was a buttoned-down professional and I made sure not to let anyone see "the real me," or what made me tick. At the time, it was not acceptable for a professional woman to show any sign of emotion in the workplace. If you did, you would be dismissed as a weak, hysterical female. Trust me, I knew long before this that it was not okay to show my emotions and I had hidden those away years earlier.

My life was pretty good. I had all the things I thought one was supposed to have. I had a nice house and a car, and I went out for dinner regularly with my then-partner. We had lots of friends, and we travelled. On the inside, though, as the years rolled forward, I became a bigger and bigger mess until, Oh Heavens! I realized I didn't have anything handled at all! The stress growing inside me was unbelievable. And I began to believe there must be something wrong with me. "*Look at everyone else,*" I'd think. "*They have everything handled. Clearly, I'm just not as bright as others. Clearly, I'm not supposed to have the life I have always envisioned.*

"And, clearly," I thought, "*I'm not 'worth' the same as the people around me.*" How could I be? Look at them! Can you see how these two very different sides of my life…the outside and the inside…led me to feel like a *fraud*? They occupy opposite ends of the scale.

Another reason I felt like a fraud was because I no longer felt like the real me inside. I had been told repeatedly how to behave, or how not to behave, and it all went completely against my instincts. To the point where I doubted them. And I doubted me. After all, I simply wanted to be loved. I didn't feel loved or loveable because of the criticism and manipulation thrown my way: I had been teased and told to be quiet as a child and I had undergone a long series of experiences that I interpreted as meaning I was unlikeable and unlovable. I chose as a partner a man who reinforced those negative beliefs. They had become comfortable, but they didn't make me feel at all happy. This is often what we call our programming. I had been programmed to believe I was just not good enough. We can't blame any one person for any of that. But we can invite others to be kinder going forward. What it meant for me at the time was that the harder I tried to be loved, to do better, and to be better, the more of a mess I became. My life was hollow because I could no longer remember who I was or who I had been. My light had dimmed so much I was in the darkness, the shadows of my life.

You might be thinking at this moment: "*Well, hold on! Angela's life doesn't seem that bad.*" And on one level, you're right. But my way of thinking, feeling, and processing pushed me far into the shadows of my own life. I truly thought I was the most unworthy person on the planet. I felt like I couldn't do anything right, no matter how hard I tried. The energy I was expending to stay in the shadows and hide myself from the world and—truly—from *me*, was exhausting.

It took its toll on me physically, emotionally, and mentally. And, if you've ever been there, too, you'll know how debilitating that is.

And it didn't make one lick of sense to me. As I mentioned, I'm a designated accountant. I have spent many years in this profession. I have my own business and I assist not-for-profit organizations as their director of finance. I have been responsible for multi-million-dollar budgets and have always felt very comfortable and competent in my role within the organizations I worked with. For many years, however, I did not have *my household financial situation* handled. It was hard for me to reconcile how I could have these two opposite experiences happening at the same time.

Feeling Like a Fraud

I remember being part of a conversation at a social event once, where someone commented that, because I was an accountant, I no doubt had my retirement savings plan completely maxed out and our finances must be spot on. I was able to just smile and not respond, allowing everyone listening to draw their own conclusions. Nothing could have been further from the truth.

The conversation made me feel, yet again, like a fraud. After all, I was an accountant, and I *should be* on top of my personal finances and have them handled. I felt that to my core. I felt incredibly inadequate—and to be honest, worth-less—because this wasn't the case. I could keep the organizations I worked for running like a well-oiled machine, but at home? Not at all. And I took complete responsibility for this embarrassing situation. Naturally, as the accountant in the house, I should be the one to manage the finances. Expertly. And wrapped in pretty paper with a bow on top.

Here is a little dose of reality for a lot of people: running the finances of an organization is totally different from running those of a household. In an organization, one can set parameters and measure against them. If adjustments must be made, then they can be taken care of. In an organization, the thorny topic of "wants" does not come into play. No one goes shopping unless the finance department okays the idea. Everything is measured against a budget and there is no deviation without a lot of conversation. There is a strict process for decision making. If things go sideways and the organization faces a worst-case scenario, then the team must cut costs and it could mean someone is laid off for a time, or completely let go. Could you see doing that in your household? Firing someone? Okay…I'm sure there *are* times you might want to do that, but, really, overspending is not necessarily the most common cause of that thought most of the time.

In our household finances, "wants" come into play to a much larger degree. Have you ever been out shopping and found that perfect pair of shoes you didn't need but you bought them anyway? We do it without thinking and without any conversation or thought around how it fits into our financial plan. We want it so we buy it. What happens when there is more than just you in your household and the other person is spending without any knowledge or concern of what your household financial situation really is, or how the household finances work?

This is double the trouble because the lack of awareness means spending happens easily and it increases the overall stress of trying to make ends meet. When spending by either party gets out of control an even bigger conversation is required as now you will need to talk to your partner, spouse, or significant other to try and solve the issue. If *you* are the over-spender, then maybe the idea of a conversation is uncomfortable so you hide it in the background hoping you can fix the overspending. This adds to our stress, too: we feel we don't have things handled and we feel we are worth-less. Another difference between managing the finances of an organization and those of a household is that everything in an organization is out in the open and discussed. There are no personal ties to anything and no one's feelings get hurt in any dollar-related conversations.

Everything is about facts, not emotions. Everything "is what it is," and people make spending decisions more or less objectively. What I have found to be true in the realm of personal finances is that people would far rather talk about what goes on in their bedroom than what goes on in their financial life. And our finances mirror our mindset. If our mindset in life is one of scarcity and struggle, then money must follow that lead. We will experience struggle in managing our finances and typically our focus on scarcity will hold them in a place where there never seems to be "enough." And the more we focus on these attributes, the more it will play out.

Okay, that was a mouthful, wasn't it? Let's try a little exercise here. When you hear or think about *personal* finances, how do you feel? Did your stomach just jump into your throat? Did your stomach clench? Or did a wave of dread flow through you?

Next part of the exercise: how do you feel when you read the following,

"You need to discuss your household finances with your significant other."

Do you feel happy and excited? Or do you feel full of anxiety and dread? Do you feel like you would like to run away and hide?

Well, for me back in the day, I would do anything to *not* have a money-related conversation with my then-partner and I got quite good at avoiding it. I tried to make things work in any way possible because I didn't want to admit out loud I didn't have it all handled. Because to do that—in my mind at the time—meant I was stupid, incompetent, and a fraud. So, trust me, I get the anxiety you may be feeling with regards to this subject. I'll let you in on a little secret. Even though I felt like this, inside I always had a feeling—mind you, it was buried deep—that there had to be more to *life*, more than being mired in these games of hide and seek, there had to be more to *me*.

I was completely enveloped in the shadows, and I had truly lost who I was…but I've learned it is possible to come out the other side of that, and stand in the light, and remember who you are. I did it, and if you've been struggling at all with standing tall in who you are, then that's my dream for you, too.

What I didn't realize at the time was that the comments and judgements other people make about us are none of our concern and none of our business, because we have no control over them. The only thing that *is* our business is how we feel and what we think. *Those* we can control.

I've learned through personal experience that if you feel unworthy and unloved, and that you don't matter, your finances will reflect those feelings. How can you have an abundant cash flow if you don't feel you deserve it? Those negative thoughts and energies actually limit your finances because they limit you. You may have heard a saying I heard a lot when I was a kid: "A watched pot never boils."

This saying also applies to your bank account. If you keep watching it and saying, "Oh my God, there is not enough!" then nothing is going to change because you are just attracting more of the same. The beauty of it all, however, is that you have the ability to change how you think and you can move in a different direction.

You can stop the feeling of being a fraud and you can start being all of *you* by fully choosing to be who you really are at your heart base— your inner most self where you are authentically you. Being all of you is an amazing way to live. From there, your overarching choice points are joy and happiness instead of scarcity and fear. When we live in *that* place, all aspects of our lives open, and we can live a life we desire and deserve because we are showing up as the best version of ourselves.

Throughout this book I will give you a number of keys to *Living Out Loud* and transforming your life so you can stop living in the shadows and begin living a life of unlimited possibilities. Please read them and take them to heart. And then read them again. It might help to download the entire list that I've prepared for you and made available on my website at www.angelaunlimited.com.

Angela's Design Keys to Living Out Loud

Key #1
You are worthy and you are unique, so embrace all of you. Becoming courageously aware of where you are right now in your life, your finances, and your thoughts, is key. From this place, you can change your whole world. It starts by getting clear and choosing you.

For my personal message
Scan the QR Code with your smart phone
Or go to: https://youtu.be/fouNqagX_Ls

Chapter Two

Judgement: A Shadow Game

*Judgement of ourselves and others stems from fear.
Fear lives in the shadows, not the light.*
—Angela Wilson

When I was a little girl, the other kids called me Big Bertha in the schoolyard. I was head and shoulders taller than all the girls and most of the boys all the way through elementary school. I had a target on my back for teasing and judging. What's more, as a little girl, family members, people at school, and people in my community told me time and again that I was too loud, and I talked too much. When I was in Grade Six my teacher yelled at me in the middle of a baseball diamond for being too loud. He told me to be quiet and he said, "I'm sick of hearing your foghorn mouth."

Can you image yelling at and centering out a 12-year-old girl who already feels like she doesn't fit in *right in the middle of the schoolyard?* It was devastating and it made me protect myself against it happening again. I made sure I quieted myself. I started to laugh less and play with less enthusiasm. My encouragement of other team members changed from open cheers to quiet congrats. I'm sure if you were to ask that teacher today if they remember this event their answer would be, "no." But all these years later, *I* remember. That is the key…I remember it.

Like many little girls, after a while I took the mean comments slung my way from these and other directions to heart, and my own inner chatter started chiming in whenever I did something imperfectly. I became my own worst nightmare: I began to bully myself.

So, the question I invite you to ask yourself is this: Who is judging you the most? Is the judgement you feel coming from your inner chatter? Or is it coming from other people in your life? Or is it coming from society as a whole? When we can pinpoint the source of those judgements, we can make a choice about whether or not to engage them. As I mentioned earlier, other people's opinions or judgements of us are really none of our business. I used to be concerned about what others thought of me because, quite frankly, I wanted to fit in. I wanted people to like me. I wanted to be loved. My inner chatter told me people judged me because I was none of the above. So, I became very good at judging myself before anyone else got the chance to do so.

By "inner chatter" I mean the loud voice you have in your head. Some would call it your ego or your egoic voice. Our inner chatter speaks to us using mainly negative words and it can be quite loud and quite critical. My inner chatter can take me from standing tall to being in a melted puddle on the bathroom floor in under ten seconds if I let it.

Our inner chatter is a tool we use to judge ourselves. It can also be the lens through which we filter what others are saying to us. So, in essence, it helps us judge *perceived* judgements. Some might ask if others really judge us or if it's our filters—the lenses which perceive the words as judgements—that are to blame. It really is fascinating when you start to get curious about inner chatter and break it down into its component parts.

JUDGEMENT: A SHADOW GAME | 17

Through my journey I have felt judged on many fronts—because I wasn't as smart as others or because of my height and weight. I can now look back and realize that all those feelings of being judged resulted from the fear I felt inside. Think about a sparkly little three-year-old girl who was a little firecracker. A complete going concern. Laughing, playing, and having fun. What that little girl wanted most of all was to be loved, to fit in, and to be happy. Judgements pushed that unlimited little girl into the shadows. Over time, she learned that being herself meant she didn't fit in; being herself endangered her ability to be loved, and because she felt she wasn't worthy, she wasn't happy. Does any of that resonate with you? The impact of judgement is extraordinary.

What do you think happens to a little girl who over time feels judged and in turn internalizes those judgements, thus making her inner chatter more critical and devastating? Well, if she is unable to stop the process, what happens is, she becomes an adult woman who is paralyzed inside herself. Not knowing which way to turn, what to say, or how to act. Of course, all of this goes on inside because on the outside she can't let anyone know for *fear* of more judgement and the *fear* of everyone thinking she is pathetic, so they will want to walk away from her.

When you are in this spiral of wanting to be loved, and fear is running the show, you are wide open for getting into a relationship with someone who, over time, finds these internal self-esteem issues and starts becoming the new bully and judge. This heightens the devastating and critical inner chatter. Have you ever felt like this? Have you ever repeated in your head what you wanted to say a minimum of ten times before you said it out loud because you didn't want to seem stupid, and you didn't want to embarrass the person you were with? I have, and it is exhausting! It is not an acceptable way to live, and I can tell you from the other side that you deserve better!

School years are a very impressionable time for girls. It really does form a lot of what will carry us through our 20s, 30s, and possibly our 40s, if not our entire life. When you are told you are not capable, or you are fat, stupid, or you-name-it, after a while that is what you start to believe. Those labels aren't reality, but they are what you see when you look in the mirror. Young girls are judged about their body size. I know, I was, all the way from kindergarten to university. Somewhere along the line I took over for myself.

Grappling with Adrenal Fatigue

Feeling fear related to judgement has a stranglehold on us and it takes a huge toll on the physical you, the emotional you, the real you. The impact this had on me was that I gained a lot of weight and put my body under constant pressure and stress. Over time it led to adrenal fatigue, stomach issues, and inflammation. Adrenal fatigue occurs when the adrenals have been overworked from being under excessive stress for a long period of time. They stop functioning at optimal levels. And because they have produced excess cortisol for an extended period they get to a point where they cannot produce enough to keep up with the stress.

Eventually I reached a breaking point: I was an emotional basket case. I could barely hold myself together. And I did because, again, on the outside I didn't want others to know how "damaged" I was. Yep, damaged was a word my inner chatter liked to judge me with as it kept me in a place of fear, smallness, and restraint. The true authentic me forgot who I was because I hid me away and protected myself through massive layers of protection. At every turn I felt hurt, and the fear of being hurt further was too much. So, I protected the real me in a cage in my heart so no one could get to me and damage me more.

The layers of protection I am referring to, which I will discuss in more detail throughout the book, were essentially like a cocoon made of layers of invisible blankets I wrapped around myself to create a place to hide. They acted as my armour to shield me from hurt. This helped me keep my guard up until I thought it was safe to allow a person to get to know me. Even then, there was an inner part almost no one managed to access. Even though I didn't want to be alone, I was too scared to let anyone in. I couldn't let them know what I was thinking or let them know the degree to which I was guarding myself.

Here's an interesting little side story on the Big Bertha teasing I experienced. About six years ago I decided to really dive into the journey of remembering who I was at my heart. Oh boy, was it time! I did this by participating in a few coaching programs and one of my most influential guides was an Awakening mentor by the name of Jennifer Hough. One day I was sitting with other people in one of Jennifer's groups and we were enjoying some deep conversations when one of the ladies mentioned her mother's name was Bertha. I hadn't heard that name for years, perhaps even several decades.

What do you think happened? Well, my insides went cold, the little girl inside of me went numb, and the adult me fought back tears like you would not believe. I had an instant visceral response to the name. Later, in a private conversation, I realized that when we don't deal with things, and shove them down inside us instead, man, they can jump out at us when we least expect it and ask to be dealt with. As I spoke my feelings out loud, I felt great relief. The pain from the teasing, all those years ago released itself from my body and I could see how I no longer had to carry it around with me. By speaking about the teasing, I released its hold over me. It had been hiding out in my subconscious all those years and was part of the foundation for my incredible cruel inner chatter. I highly recommend speaking these things out loud and freeing yourself.

I recently read in Elizabeth Gilbert's book *Big Magic* that your ego can be hurt but your soul cannot be.[1] So, when judgements hurt us, that hurt is a response from our ego, not a truth. What if we instead

---

[1] Elizabeth Gilbert, Big Magic, Creative Living Beyond Fear, Riverhead Books, An imprint of Penguin Random House LLC, New York, 2015, page 258.

shrugged off the judgements like we do our coats when we come in from outside? How do you think that would change your life, your outlook? Do you think it is possible? The answer is a resounding, YES, it is possible! Will it be easy? Not at first. But over time, as you practice listening to your heart—your real knowing—it will get ever easier.

I'm going to backtrack here for a moment. I have used the phrases, "listening to your heart," "your inner knowing," "the authentic me," and "the real me." I want to clarify what I mean by these terms. The idea of listening to my heart goes along with the idea of inner knowing. You will also see me use the phrase, "heart voice." From my perspective, this is the voice that comes from within, and not from your head. For me, it is a whisper and a knowing that what I'm feeling is real and not something my inner chatter is making up or badgering me about. Some might call the little voice inside your intuition. Inner knowing is your inner guidance system, your intuition. Some might even say your "higher levels" are speaking to you. You might have a different word or sense based on your belief system. To me, being the authentic me means being fully me and not morphing myself in any way—standing fully as Angela in all aspects. I believe when you are living as the authentic you, you also stand in integrity and alignment with who you are supposed to be. When you are living in that space you are the real you.

A mentor of mine has a saying: "Be yourself or don't. Others will judge you either way. But if you choose to express *all of you* into the world, at least ONE of you will be happy." When I first heard this, I was all, "*Like What*?!" I heard the words, but I couldn't quite grasp them. Five years later I get it. Honestly, I would rather be happy than worry about what everyone else is saying about me. I will admit that, at times, I still fall into the trap of letting the judgements in. After all, I am human. But now they don't linger as long or have the same effect on me as they did back in the day.

A great way to determine if judgements coming your way are something you should listen to is to give them the five-year test. That is, if what is being said will impact your life in five years then it is something to listen to. If it won't, then it's time to let it slip away and turn your focus elsewhere. You get to choose to listen or not. Your choice! If you think it will have a *real* impact on your life (i.e., life-altering) you get to choose how to deal with it and what if anything needs to be changed. I would invite you to sit with this and not make a hasty decision. I like to journal to work these types of things out. I find putting pen to paper allows ideas to flow out of me and I have worked out many a thought, situation, or feeling this way. Try letting your thoughts around the judgement pour onto the page. You can always burn it or shred it later if you want to make sure no one will see it. I would suggest you not censor what you are writing—just write.

Over our time and our journey, and through our experiences, we can learn how to handle judgement. It is an ongoing battle for some. I, personally, would love it if the kids of today never had to worry about it. Never had to think about it. What a world it would be, if kids could just be kids, and not get taught by others around them how to judge. What if instead they learned to embrace each other for their uniqueness and what each of them brings to the world? To learn that they will not be judged as "failures." Actually, nothing would be seen as a failure because everyone would be out there trying things and expressing their authentic selves. Now *that* vision makes my heart sing!

I'm going to end here with a quote from Theodore Roosevelt.

"It is not the critic who counts; not the man who points out how the strong man stumbles, or where the doer of deeds could have done them better. The credit belongs to the man who is actually in the arena, whose face is marred by dust and sweat and blood; who strives valiantly; who errs, who comes short again and again because there is no effort without error and shortcoming; but who does actually strive to do the deeds; who knows the great enthusiasms, the great devotions; who spends himself in a worthy cause; who at the best knows in the end the triumph of high achievement, and who at the worst, if he fails, at least fails while daring greatly, so that his place shall never be with those cold and timid souls who neither know victory nor defeat. "[2]

I love this quote because it basically says that if you aren't out there giving your all then your opinion, and your judgements, are of less significance than those of the people who have the courage to stand up and live fully. It is way too easy to sit on the sidelines of life and judge people. Let's not be like that.

---

[2] Theodore Roosevelt speech "Citizenship in a Republic" given at the Sobonne in Paris on April 23, 1910

Angela's Design Keys to Living Out Loud

Key #2
You need to be you. It is imperative. Other people's judgements of you do not define you and they are none of your business. Let them be them and you be you. It sounds simple but it is a huge challenge, and it takes practice. You have the courage to do this. Just listen to your heart rather than to your inner chatter.

For my personal message
Scan the QR Code with your smart phone
Or go to: https://youtu.be/IDvj4HMJbfE

Chapter Three

Losing Your Voice

*It seemed like losing my voice happened easily
and in a heartbeat. Gaining it back was hard
but oh-so-worth it.*
—Angela Wilson

My Turning Point, came when the man I had been living with turned to me and said, "I think I'm leaving you." In that moment, the world as I knew it ceased to exist. I was devastated, numb, and confused. At first my well-practiced habit of proving myself kicked in and I tried to show what an exemplary partner I could still be. Then I blamed myself to the point of considering not being on the planet anymore.

At the time, I had no idea who I was or how I was ever going to move forward and a friend of mine said, "okay girl it is time for you to go and take this two-day seminar a friend of mine puts on. It's called *Get Out of Your Own Way*. It's time for you to snap out of where you are." I said I would look into it. In the back of my mind, I was skeptical, as I knew nothing about the seminar or the person hosting it, but I trusted the friend recommending it. Her and I had gotten our accounting designations together and became great friends, so I knew she wouldn't steer me wrong. I looked it up and to my surprise I found the next session was going to take place fairly close to where I lived in just a week's time. It would be several months before another one would be held in my area. I didn't want to spend the money, as not only had I lost my voice, but I had lost my perspective at that time of what I could afford.

And I signed up. With great trepidation, the following Saturday morning I drove the half-hour to where the seminar was being held. I walked in, and was greeted with a warm hello, and a hug. My first thought was "OMG this person just hugged me…what the *hell*?" In those days I was not a hugger. Now I thrive on hugs and even crave them.

There were approximately a dozen people in the group. They all seemed to be chatting away and introducing themselves. I stood apart and observed. One of the participants, a woman, came over and started talking to me. I timidly engaged in the conversation, of course not wanting to give anything about myself away, but I was raised to always be polite to people. What was happening with me on the inside was private. You didn't talk about such things with strangers—or anyone, for that matter. I found myself a seat, not knowing at the time that it was right beside the chair of the facilitator, Jennifer, who would later become an important mentor and friend, as I mentioned earlier.

The seminar started with lots of discussion and sharing. I felt like a little mouse who was trying to hide in plain sight from the hawk circling above. My inner chatter was soooo loud and the messages it was sending to me were so hurtful that I sank into my chair even further, hoping it would envelope me and I would go unnoticed. By the end of the first day, my mind was reeling from all I had taken in and everything the other participants had shared.

Suddenly, the facilitator turned to me and said, "okay my quiet, little one, it is time for you to speak." I was terrified, but in my heart,

I knew if I didn't open up and let my voice out, it might be gone forever. I hesitated, then started talking, and to my surprise, and even a bit of horror, everyone listened. No one was asking me to be quiet and no one was ignoring me. I didn't feel judged. Instead, I felt heard and for the first time in an extremely long time I could hear my true voice sneaking out to test the light. I have never forgotten that day. Nor do I think I ever will. At the same time, for the first time in decades, I could feel my heart whisper to me that it was okay, to just believe, and to be vulnerable for a moment. I'm glad I listened because it was the real start to using my authentic voice.

I met some lovely women that day. I also learned that when I used my voice, others did listen. By allowing my voice to shine through, people saw me—and even if they saw only a snippet of me, they saw me. A wonderful woman came over to me toward the end of the second day and hugged me. She told me how strong I was and how capable I was, which honestly shocked me, because I didn't feel either of those at the time.

After the hug, she gave me a bracelet she was wearing. It had been given to her by a dear friend whose life was ending, and the words embossed upon it were "Friend For Life." She told me to wear it and remember her. The bracelet would assist my courage going forward, she said, as her friend had been an amazing person and would want her to give the bracelet to me. I was touched. I was also confused. How could this perfect stranger be so kind and say such nice things about me? After all, she had just met me the previous day.

What I realized, in that moment, was that because I had let my voice shine through, she had gained an insight into me. She saw me and wanted to assist me. I still have that bracelet and every time I see it, I think of her and that moment. Actually, I'm wearing it right now as it symbolizes the start of using my voice and the start of remembering who I am at a heart level.

I ran into this same woman a couple of times after that. When she saw me, she would give me a big hug. She would ask how I was and if I still had the bracelet. The exchanges always amazed me because of the warmth and the caring this woman exuded. Just as she had had an impact on me that day, I had impacted her as well. I would never have imagined how choosing to use my voice would impact others as well as myself.

The other benefit of attending the program was that taking a leap of faith towards the idea I was worth spending the money on required me to really listen to my inner knowing and find help to move me forward. That investment was the start of my journey to here. Even today I believe it is important to invest in and believe in ourselves.

It's funny, as I wrote the title to this chapter—"Losing Your Voice"—I snickered to myself because it sounds like I'm going to talk about laryngitis and how to recover from it. Interestingly enough, it could almost be seen that way. During the lost years of my life, I never completely stopped talking, as that was not an option—we must communicate with others—even though on the inside I wished I could. It was the way I engaged in conversation and the times when I was completely quiet that were the issue. Have you ever been out for an evening and thought to yourself, *"I haven't said anything in about half an hour and no one has noticed"*? It happened to me a lot. As I mentioned earlier, sometimes I would play a game to see how long it would take for someone to bring me back into the conversation, or to even notice I was being quiet.

But it really wasn't a great game. It fed my inner chatter's assertion that I didn't matter. It was a dark time for me as by that point I had basically withdrawn inward, and conversation was difficult at the best of times. I would go over what I wanted to say a minimum of ten times in my head before I said it out loud because I had given my power away to the judgements and opinions of the people around me. After all, everyone else was smarter and more talented than I was. At least it was my perception that they were but, unfortunately, I had heard a lot about how inferior I was by this time, and I had bought in to that belief.

Trust me, over the years I would sometimes scream at myself in my head, JUST STAND UP. JUST BE WHO YOU ARE. But how do you do that when you feel you are continually shut down, ignored, or dismissed? Well, what I did was let others be right. Let others be in control. Let others have all the power over my life. My voice curled up inside of me, in the protective cage I built. It buried itself deep under a mountain of protective layers. We'll talk about those layers later, but for now just picture a mountain of blankets piled on top of me, wrapped around me. Have you ever felt that if you screamed at the top of your lungs no one would hear you?

What do you think it does to a person when they lose their voice?

What has it done to you?

Okay, let's take a step back because even though it felt like I had gotten to that space in a heartbeat I had really edged into it over several decades…bit by bit, snippet by snippet. It wasn't as though one day I was using my voice and the next day I wasn't. It was like waves washing over pebbles making them smooth or sand pouring onto a rock and wearing a hole in it. Have you experienced this? My guess is you have—or something similar—because you're reading this book.

"Be Quiet and Stop Talking"

So, where did this start? My best recollection is that I started to learn my voice was not to be heard while I was at school. I mentioned earlier about the Baseball Incident but, actually, I often heard people telling me to be quiet and to stop talking. But that was only one of a multitude of messages I received that amounted to the idea I got that being me was not okay. An interesting aside…when I was younger—

around Grade 5—I actually entered public speaking contests. You see, at the time I wasn't afraid to talk in front of people.

But eventually, I lost my voice.

What I really lost was the use of the voice that came from my authentic self. I lost me. I ran away and hid inside. I didn't speak up because when I did, I was judged for not being bright enough, not using the correct words, for being unsophisticated. I often felt no one listened to what I had to say, or they dismissed me. And, certainly, when I was with a former partner, if I couldn't back up an opinion without all the documented proof on why I was right or justified, he would dismiss me for being simple, unread, or not having a real opinion.

And so, the judgement that surrounded me contributed to losing my voice and it also made my fear of being unloved and alone skyrocket. It made me doubt my every move. The fear inside me was massive, and tangible, and I felt paralyzed inside. Have you ever felt like it would be a blessing to be swallowed whole by some enormous nameless monster? The pivotal time after my partner left was horrible, and turned out to be the best thing that could have happened to me. Because that's when I started to regain my voice. It took several years, but I finally found my voice again, and I'm using it in numerous ways today—including in this book—in hopes of being of assistance to others.

For a long time, I thought I would never be able to write a book, partly because I had been told my whole life long how bad I was in English, and that I couldn't write well. Someone even told me at one point they were going to give me a bucket of commas as a gift. I believed I was a bad writer, and, in those days, I thought my voice was unimportant. I wanted to yell, "Look at me, I have value!" But I could only do that in my head and even my head told me to be quiet. In my heart, though, I knew I wanted to write a book.

When I decided to take this venture on, I worked with a book mentor/coach. She is such a wonderful person. Her name is Susan Crossman of Crossman Communications. When we started talking about it, I explained I wasn't sure because I had always been told I wasn't good at writing. I told her the old stories I just mentioned, and her response was, "Angela, that's what editors are for. *Everybody* has an editor!" It made perfect sense. It also made sense because I now realize we are all unique, and we each have unique skills. We fall into the stressful trap of perfectionism and expect ourselves to be superhuman and able to do everything. But I don't have to be good at everything, and neither do you, my friend. Just be the best version of you, and let others be the best version of them. All of our geniuses will interlink.

Your voice holds great wisdom and in turn holds great power. When we communicate from our authentic heart, we are expressing ourselves fully. We are giving voice to our inner knowing, our inner compass, the guidance that allows us to communicate the essence of who we are. And if we don't use our voice, aren't we robbing the world of our uniqueness?

Know that your voice doesn't have to be lost forever. It can be, if that is your choice. You may have hidden your voice for a different reason than I did. One thing I know in my heart is that not using my voice, and listening to my loud inner chatter instead, was torture. It was out of alignment with my true self, and it had a huge impact on me mentally, physically, and emotionally. And I had completely hidden my spiritual side.

You can only carry on so long doing that until there is some catalyst to either snap you out of it or to confirm that for the time being you are going to stay where you are. The catalyst for me was the end of an intimate relationship and as hard as it was, I chose to move forward. This meant starting to use my voice regardless of how scared I was and regardless of what I had been told about myself. For the first time in a very long time, I could, on occasion, hear the whisper of my heart guiding me.

A lot of relationships don't start out in a problematic way, they may grow into it over time as your self-esteem diminishes and you use your voice less and less.

What I know deep down, and have learned even more through my journey, is that controlling, manipulative, bullying, and abusive (emotionally or physically) relationships, regardless of whom that relationship is with, are not okay. A spotlight needs to be shone on these issues even more and they need to be brought out into the open.

I personally know several friends, colleagues, and clients including myself that have encountered these types of relationships (manipulative or toxic) in their lives. The unfortunate part is, many feel they have brought it on themselves or that it is justified. This happens because they have allowed themselves to be diminished, which brings about shame, fear, doubt, a sense of being worth-less. This leads them to losing who they are, feeling judged at every syllable that they utter, and living in fear because of their self-doubt. This is unfortunate because it was not and is not their fault.

When someone steps up and uses what they perceive as a weakness in you, against you intentionally to make you feel small, to manipulate you into doing what they want, or to think the way they want you to think, that is wrong. We need to stop tolerating that behaviour in our society. Lots of times it is done so subtly (not physically) that the person in it doesn't even realize what has happened until they are out of the situation.

When you have lost your voice, certain words and situations may still trigger you at times as occasionally happens to me. However, as time goes on the impact will significantly decrease. My work has been to take steps every day to be unapologetically me. To be the best version of me, which means using my voice and not silencing it.

I know that it can be terrifying to start to use your voice, but I urge you to try and, little by little, as you test it out, you will see it's okay to use your authentic voice and let the world see you. Not using your voice keeps you in the shadows. It keeps you living in fear. Yep…it is scary if you think several steps down the road at what using your voice might look like, so I encourage you not to look too many steps ahead.

Just identify a step you can take right now and take it. I remember reading a quote once that pointed to the idea that if you had to be able to see what was beyond every curve before you went out in your car you would never drive at night or never drive at all. Just start taking steps to be you and let yourself be heard. It is a process for sure and it is a marathon, not a sprint. I still at times soften my voice because I'm a little unsure of myself but I never hide it anymore. We are meant to live our lives being heard and being seen and they go hand in hand.

For me, part of the process of finding my voice again involved allowing new people into my life. I realized along the journey that I didn't have to be alone. I realized it was okay to allow myself to be seen and once I started using my voice, I couldn't help but be seen. What I discovered is that it opened up a whole new way of life. I was no longer mentally exhausted after conversations and the conversations I have now are incredible because they are full of substance, and they are with people who aren't afraid to be seen.

I have never felt more alive than I do at this juncture in my life. I'm fulfilling a dream by writing this book. I'm also fulfilling a dream of being of assistance to others by allowing my voice to be heard. I didn't do this by myself, nor could I have, because we are meant to be in a community of people who see you, hear your voice, and remind you who you really are at your authentic heart whenever you forget. In fact, that's part of the assistance my company, Angela Unlimited, provides.

Start by testing your voice out in a safe space. A safe space is where you feel comfortable you won't be judged. This might be with one person at first or a in small group. I encourage you to get your voice into the room. The key is to not censor it. Speak from your heart. I would suggest that afterwards you write down how it felt and what your reaction was. By doing this over time you can see evidence of how much you have grown and expanded. Also, make sure you celebrate that you took that step. It is a big one! I would also encourage you to write down what you said, if you can remember. If not, write down whatever you *can* remember. Have a look at it. Is the language you are using positive or negative? If negative, rephrase it into positive wording. This will assist you to lift yourself to a different level of being.

When we use positive words and raise our awareness of them, more positive experiences and possibilities come to us. Positive attracts positive and negative attracts negative. I use the exercise of rephrasing with my clients. At first it often amazes them how many of their thoughts are negative. What they find is that after doing this for a while their days are brighter, and their moods are lighter. They also notice life becomes less hard, less transactional. Try the simple exercise above and see where your thoughts are taking you!

Angela's Design Keys to Living Out Loud

Key #3
Your voice is your special gift. It is meant to be used not quieted. People who try to quiet us have their own agendas. Live out loud as all of you every day, in every minute. Remember: when we all live as our authentic selves our geniuses will interlink. So be you and shine!

For my personal message
Scan the QR Code with your smart phone
Or go to: https://youtu.be/mIBwVeLZizk

Chapter Four

The Protective Layers We Wrap Around Us

The layers of armour we swirl ourselves in interweave and overlap. They cocoon us and make us feel safe. But as they thicken and multiply, they dim us, shield us, and bury us, until it's hard to breathe.
—Angela Wilson

My husband stopped me in my tracks recently during a conversation in which I was discussing how out of sorts I was feeling. At times, I have an overwhelming sense of aloneness and separateness and I've come to realize this comes from the protective armour I put in place over the years to help me cope with my life, to stay separate and apart, so I could feel like an island in the stream, or a fish out of water.

"That's a place you feel comfortable," he said.

Say what?!

At first, I wanted to protest but I couldn't because it was oh-so-true. I had let that well-woven dense layer become so cozy it was there in an instant without me even having to think about it or summon it. Without having to invoke it or consciously wrap myself in it. I've sat with that feeling for a couple of weeks now not knowing where it was going to go or how I was going to move forward with it. Would it come along like the old friend I knew, or would we greet each other in a new way? The answer came to me finally: it was time for my relationship with my protection to change and grow.

Soldiers wear armour to protect themselves during battle and in medieval times it consisted of heavy metal plates, chainmail, and leather protectors. Can you feel the heaviness of it all? And how difficult it must have been to move, or even breathe, while wearing your armour? Well, I wasn't wearing physical armour, but with all the protective layers with which I had surrounded myself, I might as well have been. A sword would have been able to penetrate easily. But I was shielding myself from the weaponry of words, wielded by others and by me. It's part of why words are now so important to me, and why certain innocuous words can crumble me still.

When people say you are "not that bright," or you are "fat," "stupid," "not that pretty," "loud," "not capable," "a princess," and much more besides, it's hard *not* to take it all in. I did. And every time these slights were hurled at me, I would weave yet another layer of protection around me. I thought if I could wrap myself in an invisible blanket, nothing would hurt. Everything would be okay. I could survive. Maybe I could cope. Over 30-odd years I wrapped and cocooned myself in layers of protective insulation. I became masterful at it as the years progressed. I thought it would stop the pain and it gave me a sense of security and a feeling of control. With each new hurt, slight, tease, or judgement I added more layers, their density amplifying my feelings of being protected, while increasingly muffling my voice.

You might be wondering why I felt I needed these protective layers, or you might be nodding and saying, "I get it."

I didn't start out to try and protect myself and I didn't intentionally at first start to integrate these layers into my being. Initially, it was more like I withdrew a bit as words and phrases pelted me like stones. Yes, I would lash back at times but most of the time that just made it all worse. Instead, I started piecing my armour together to protect myself. They couldn't hurt me if I just grew thicker skin. Have you heard the old saying, "you better toughen up and grow a thicker skin if you are going to be out in the world?" But why should we have to do that? Why shouldn't we be able to just be ourselves and live our lives expressing ourselves fully, while shining our light? Why did I feel I had to protect myself against all the hurts that were happening? To be honest, I doubt most people had any clue how far down I was buried. I know I didn't realize what was happening, and it still shocks me sometimes as I move through my journey today, and peel away the layers in which I sought refuge.

These protective layers—or what some people call protective mechanisms—keep us perceptively safe. They help our ego to cope in the world, or at least that's what my inner chatter told me. You see, as the number of layers continued to mount, so did my inner chatter because I thought at the time it was also there to protect me. What a wrong idea that was. Can you see how confused I was? I thought, in a strange way, that my inner chatter was trying to keep me safe.

Unfortunately, it put me in a depleted state: I had the notion that if I were hard on myself, and beat myself down, then the insults and judgements of others would have less impact on me. But here's the part I hadn't counted on: what I was actually getting instead of protection was a double whammy. Now I was getting hit from outside of myself *and* from within. I have a feeling you might know a thing or two about this yourself.

What do your protective layers—your layers of armour—look like? I'll give you a side story of mine from three or four years ago. My husband commented one day that when we went certain places, he could see me change as we drew closer to our destination. I sat differently. I spoke differently. It's like I started to steel myself. I remember saying to him "I had no idea you could see that." He smiled. As I stopped and thought for just a second, I realized, of course he could notice these things because he sees me, the real me, at my heart level. It was fascinating. I knew I had come quite a long way, but I hadn't realized I still had those layers hiding around me, ready to jump into action. We are each a work in progress.

Do you think if you've had your protective layers in place for many years you can completely get rid of them? Would you want to? I don't think they ever truly go away because they have become part of us. However, as we go through our journey, if we choose to allow ourselves to open and to be seen, things have to change. If they don't, then we stay locked in the middle of a constant tug of war between our protection and our knowing. That battle takes its toll on us because it isn't a battle we are supposed to have to endure.

When we were born, we didn't have these protective guardians in place. There was no armour, layers, or mechanisms. There was just us. In our knowing. We learned to embrace these guardians. They became old friends and eventually it felt like there was no separation between us. Harmful as they are, they can bring us immense comfort. They can create such a cozy spot to live and live there we can. But if we want to shine in life and be the best version of ourselves possible, then we can't remain in that cozy protected spot because while the protection may keep us safe it also doesn't let our light shine out into the world. If we are protecting against anything coming in, then the opposite is true as well…nothing can get out.

I find this topic truly fascinating as it is interwoven through all aspects of my life. It's an area of diligent progression as I choose to move forward on my journey.

What I've realized is that by continuing to embrace my protective layers I was keeping myself from truly being all of me. You can't hide and still be seen, which we will also discuss in a later chapter.

At some point, you have to decide it is time to let your protective guardians relax and breathe. You have to let them stand down from being on high alert if you want your light to shine and if you want to stop living in the shadows. Because that's what the layers do. They cast shadows and darkness. As I said, we were born into this world with all our potential at hand. But different experiences taught us to step back and shield ourselves in the shadows. When we remain in the shadows for too long, we can forget who we are at our authentic heart. The layers in which we have buried ourselves don't let the sun's golden light shine in to warm us. When we allow that light in, we can reconnect with ourselves and say…"ah, there you are."

I consider myself very blessed and fortunate because even though I adapted to this cocoon of my own making, somehow, I had left some tiny gaps and a bit of light penetrated. It came to me through a whispered knowingness…"you are meant for more." At times the whisper was…"you know there is more to life." I believe we all have a spark in us that keeps burning as we go through our journey. It's the guiding light moving us forward.

And choosing to remember who we are at our essence is one of the greatest choices we can make. We all have the strength, courage, and bravery to make this choice. It may take us a bit of time and that's okay because it's the constant choosing that moves us forward, that changes our relationship to our protective guardians, and dissolves the shadows.

Just before my final thought on this subject I would like you to take five minutes and write down what your protective layers are. Write what they look like, feel like, smell like. Now take another five minutes and write down how you think your life would change if you didn't have these. I think you can see where I'm going with this. I want you to explore what your life might be like if you were standing strong in your life, and you had no need for protective layers.

A final thought I will leave you with regarding the protection in which we have swirled ourselves: if you wrap yourself completely in a blanket from head to foot, what part of you does the world see? It sees none of you. It only sees the blanket. From inside the blanket what do you see? Maybe a bit of light that struggles through the woven fabric—but for the most part it's dark, shadowy, and somewhat hard to breathe.

It might be scary to show the world who we are but isn't it also scary to live in that dark shadowy place and not be *you*? You have the strength to loosen the blanket and let in more light. I have found that, as I let my grip loosen, I've had the most amazing people come into my life and my life has become more of what I knew it could be. I have no doubt that as I let go of my grip completely and stand fully as my twinkling self, I'll increasingly have the sense that *this* is what life is supposed to be.

Angela's Design Keys to Living Out Loud

Key #4
Protecting yourself from hurts and fears means you are not living your life. You are hiding from your life. If we choose to live as the best version of ourselves, we have to unravel the protective layers and stand fully as who we truly are.

For my personal message
Scan the QR Code with your smart phone
Or go to: https://youtu.be/j4LVzH0OpKg

Chapter Five

Feelings of Low Self-Esteem and Low Self-Worth

Your feeling of self-worth is one of your most valuable assets. Without it, we feel worth-less. The story of being worth-less is one that needs to be rewritten. We are all unique beautiful beings who matter.
—Angela Wilson

When I was a sparkly three-year-old I remember thinking that life was completely unlimited. At that age we are still following our own inner guidance and the concept of low self-esteem or low self-worth doesn't exist. Most of us can play, laugh, create, and talk out loud without holding back. We can be purely and simply ourselves. I was quite a chatty little girl. I played outside and made up many imaginary games. This was about the time, however, when I started to learn what was expected of a little girl. When I was that age, little girls were supposed to be seen and not heard. When we were out visiting family or friends I was expected to act like a little lady and use my manners. Sitting still and refraining from talking were not my strongest suits in those days. Can you imagine how many times a little girl like me got into trouble?!

So, that's when I started learning about what was acceptable and what was not acceptable. Maybe you have your own version of this as well. I learned there was way more about me that was unacceptable than there was that was acceptable. These teachings eroded my sense of who I was. And when that erosion starts to happen, well, my friend, it is a grease-lined slippery slope down to not feeling worthy. Can you relate? By the way, the story of how I lost my self-worth is not a huge tragedy. There was no immense trauma, although there was a lot of drama that caused me to value the people involved far more than I valued myself. As a result, I *de*valued how I saw myself in the world and thus the value I brought to the table. It affected how I behaved, and how I showed up in the world.

There was never any one event or a moment in time when I suddenly felt less worthy than I had a heartbeat earlier. It was a gradual progression that started when I was around three and continued until I started my journey to remembering who I was at about age 45. That journey helped me embrace the "me" my sparkly three-year-old self was supposed to become. Let's take a meander through that timeline and see if any of this sounds familiar to you.

So, let's dive into this…as I mentioned, it starts as a young girl who is expected to be seen and not heard and for whom being quiet is almost impossible. Add, too, that I was curious and had a big imagination. It's hard to shoehorn a little girl like that into the persona of a proper little girl but that's what needed to happen. I grew up in a small community where everyone knew everyone else and there was a clear expectation that we do not embarrass our family and not be the kid others were talking about. So, the effort to fit in began, and I learned my place.

FEELINGS OF LOW SELF-ESTEEM AND LOW SELF-WORTH | 47

All the way through school the other kids teased me, and several teachers told me I didn't measure up and I wouldn't amount to much. That is hard to reconcile, when the three-year-old inside me kept thinking "I'm meant for something more." As I mentioned earlier, that was the spark inside that kept me going. It was the part of my light and sparkle that just wouldn't extinguish. It knew the truth and it was a placeholder for later.

From elementary school through high school, I heard I was

Fat
Too loud
Too big
Not as smart as others
Capable but lazy
Clumsy and uncoordinated
Not pretty
Not applying myself enough—if I did I could do better
Not good at English
Not good at French
Not good at Science
Not good at advanced Math
Not good at Art
Not coordinated enough for sports
Not built right to be a figure skater
Lacking the aptitude needed to become an accountant

And there was more. Did you hear your version of those judgements growing up? None of these criticisms on their own are too much for a little girl becoming a young woman to handle. I took all of these perceived failings in, however, and held onto them. They became the truth I measured myself against. With those concepts, words, and notions swirling around inside, how could my self-esteem and self-worth *not* suffer? All of those criticisms clearly pointed out to me that I was not enough and that others were far superior to me. You may have experienced your own version of this and, if so, my heart goes out to you. People say thoughtless things sometimes with no regard for the impact they might be having. But let's look at this as an opportunity to grow.

It was my Grade 13 accounting teacher who made the snarky comment about my lack of aptitude for accounting. Toward the end of the year, I asked my teacher about the accounting profession. I remember clearly to this day how he gave a little snort and told me not to bother because I wasn't smart enough to be an accountant. Granted, I don't remember being an A+ student, but if memory serves, I was generally a B+ or an A student.

So, picture if you can a young woman nearing the end of high school and trying to figure out what to do next and pretty much every teacher has told her, "you suck." Then I took four other advanced math classes and heard it was not for me: I was basically told that I couldn't add or subtract. My 18-year-old brain couldn't handle that one. I had no idea what I *could* become, with all the discouraging messages I took in. What would you do? Well, I thought, "*surely I can add and subtract.*" So, off to university I went to become an accountant anyway.

The road to obtaining my designation was tarnished by hard work, disappointment, and tears. Of course, it was because I doubted my abilities every step of the way. Looking at it from my 55-year-old eyes and seeing the path I took I can certainly say the reality is that I have a ton of courage, and tenacity is definitely one of my strengths. Looking back, I don't know how I persevered through it all. And at university—a rather large university—my already low self-esteem became lower. This was my first time away from home. I was excited because it felt like a fresh start. These people didn't know me so certainly I could test the waters and be me. I learned very quickly that was not going to be the case. I was paired up with a roommate in residence who truly didn't like me. I thought at first maybe we could be friends but that was not our destiny. The classes themselves were boring and had nothing to do with accounting.

During my first year I had to complete a series of general business courses with a couple of electives. I felt overloaded and overwhelmed, and I didn't even have a space where I could be me. I'm sure some of this will sound familiar to others reflecting on their first year of university. I did have one safe haven at that time because my great aunt and uncle lived not far from the university so I would escape to their home often. I had gone to school for the experience of higher education and to grow and become an adult. It felt nothing like that at all.

At the end of the first semester, I failed my first class ever. Yep… Computer Science 101 knocked me out of what I thought was to be my dream. I had never in my life failed a course. Hell, I had never gotten anything below a C before and now, out I was. You see, the school I went to accepted 2,000 students into the first-year accounting program and only 1,000 were allowed into second year. Talk about setting people up to fail! We were also routinely told that if we failed any class, we were out, no questions asked. At that point I thought of switching my major, but I didn't. Instead, I found a different route to get where I needed to go.

Right after that failure I met a man who attended a different university. During the summer after my first year, as I was trying to figure out what I was going to do with my life, he talked to the Dean of Admissions at his university to see if there was a possibility I might be accepted there. He took the chance because he had had a similar experience at the school I had attended. The Dean accepted me, and I was off again to university. One big notable difference was that the curriculum was very different, and the school was smaller. I now had a chance. I took full advantage of this opportunity itself and worked my tail off. Four years later I graduated with an Honours Bachelor of Business Administration degree majoring in Accounting. I was off to start my career…or so I thought.

Glimmers of Capability

Can you imagine where my self-esteem sat at that moment? Well, it was still low, but it had bounced back a bit. After all, I had just finished university and I had a full-time position at a big accounting firm. I should have had the world by the tail. After all, I now had a man with whom I was living and who maybe loved me., I was starting a career, and I was university-educated. But none of these cured my feelings of low self-worth. In those early years of my career, I had glimmers of what I might be capable of, or where I might fit. But I was still looking outside of myself for answers, confirming what my inside thoughts kept telling me... which was that everyone else was more significant than I was.

Next came the studying and exam process to get my accounting designation and along with them... more disappointment and more tears. I was fired twice because I failed two different exams. Maybe my Grade 13 accounting teacher was right—maybe I couldn't do this, maybe it was beyond my capabilities. Around this time, I realized I didn't want to work for an accounting firm, so I set my sights on a different accounting designation and success was mine! But the hidden damage was already done. I joined a company with a toxic work environment and worked there for almost 12 years. With each passing year my self-esteem diminished even further. I tried to find other creative things to do but each one fell short of making me feel worthy. The slights and the jabs continued from all angles, and I sunk even further into the shadows.

I moved to another job, but it only lasted a bit over a year as I had jumped from one toxic environment to another. The seedling that came out of that era, however, was that I decided it was time to work for myself and I started my own accounting practice. You would think at this point I would be on top of the moon and my feelings of self-esteem and self-worth would be amping up a bit. They did for a short while, but they soon waned because I kept thinking that sooner or later everyone was going to find out I wasn't that bright. Here's where part of the fraud analogy I mentioned previously comes in. You see, my lips were saying, "Yes, I'm capable and I can do the job," but inside my head my inner chatter was yelling "NO YOU CAN'T! How many times do you have to be told you don't measure up?" I just had to keep everything outwardly handled.

And I kept that façade up for many years. Some of those were good years and some…not so much. My self-worth was really starting to crack and crumble under the weight of trying to show I had everything handled. I kept trying different things. In the back of my mind during this time I would hear the whisper, "There has to be more…there has to be more…"

My life became increasingly sad, and my feelings of self-esteem and self-worth were in free fall. I hit rock bottom and I was on my own. My inner chatter began asking me, "Who is ever going to love you?" Have you ever had those thoughts? Have you ever thought so little of yourself that you truly thought no one would love you? After all, how could they?

Well, my friends, this was the turnaround point where my feelings of self-esteem and self-worth started to build. I was on my own and it was time to rebuild, remember, and recreate. I realized I had people in my life who believed in me, and I started to use my voice because suddenly I wasn't being told to be quiet anymore. People were listening to what I had to say. My friend, Andrée Cusson, who is the friend I mentioned I got my designation with, was instrumental in some key conversations. And it all sparked a thought: maybe I did matter! At that time, I also started to believe there was someone out there for me. My true soulmate. And in the right amount of time, I found him, my amazing partner in everything. I knew he was the man for me not long after we met because I could talk to him and I never went through what I was going to say in my head before I said it, I could just talk. Ah…using my voice became okay. Being me became okay.

True Partnership

We have been together for nine years now. I treasure every single one. He did not come into my life to save a damsel in distress or slap some emotional Band-Aids on some very deep hurts that I had not yet resolved. He came into my life once I had already been rebuilding my sense of self for quite a while. He came to be my partner in everything, and, so we could together shine our best selves out into the world. I knew where I was headed by the time I met Gord, but I wasn't sure how I was going to get there.

The key for me in building my feelings of self-worth and self-esteem was to find love and support from a variety of people, and to surround myself with people who could truly see me. Who could remind me who I was at my heart. I began to realize I wanted to one day write a book and I knew I wanted to start an organization to assist women to come out of the shadows and stand in their light. I didn't know how, but it felt like a possibility. Through the darkness of that time, I was reminded who I am at my heart because that is when my journey of remembering who I was started. It ignited the flames of self-esteem and self-worth and started fanning them.

If you are on this journey yourself, I would like to remind you there will be days when you forget or slip a bit and the old doubt about your self-worth will creep in. This happens because it has been part of you for so long. It is a learned habit. It is also important when this happens to give yourself some grace. By grace, I mean to allow yourself the patience you extend to anyone else you know who had the same slip. Tomorrow is another day, and we get a fresh start to move forward. So, no harsh talk and no inner chatter on how you messed up. Deep breath…allow others who can see you remind you that all is good. And, out of the fire will rise a phoenix.

In the old days no one could just say to me, "You are worth it" and expect me to believe it. Once you have fallen down that landslide you have to relearn who you are. I found it was helpful to have others in my corner to support me as I relearned this key piece of wisdom, but, ultimately, I got there. Only I could listen to the voice inside and make the ultimate choice to see myself as worthy. We are all worthy of our lives, our dreams, and our desires. We just sometimes forget along the way due to things we hear and take on, things that lead us into the shadow of unworthiness.

I would encourage you to increase your self-worth, your self-esteem, and to get into community with people who can see you. Even though it is uncomfortable—even scary—be yourself. This could look like joining a club or a class of some type. I met one of my closest friends at a Tai-chi class. I went not knowing a soul. We started talking. Decided to have coffee. And 25+ years later we are still friends. I would also suggest reading books that nourish your soul and lift your vibration. Most importantly, don't isolate yourself. Get out and enjoy life.

I hope this will help you. Our circumstances may have been different, but the feelings are probably relatable. The one thing I can tell you is that you are totally worthy. You might not have people in your life reminding you that you are worthy, and you yourself might be your own worst critic. I was there, too. And yet, with a lot of help from others, I shifted how I was seeing myself and have come back into a place of embracing how unique and special I am. I am worthy now and I was all along. You are, too.

Angela's Design Keys to Living Out Loud

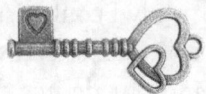

Key #5
There is only one of you on this earth. You were born worthy, and you will remain worthy for you whole journey. The gift you are is important to the world. Be you!

For my personal message
Scan the QR Code with your smart phone
Or go to: https://youtu.be/qER1D8YRr4I

Chapter Six

Proving/Mattering is not Your Job

Proving and mattering are exhausting. Bottom line: YOU MATTER! You always have and you always will. Be your magnificent self every day, all day!
—Angela Wilson

I want you to read this sentence and then close your eyes, take in a deep breath, and feel the next few words deep into your core…

You Matter! You have always mattered! You always will matter.

I know it and I want you to know it and feel it. Proving your worth and proving you matter are exhausting and you deserve better than that!

The whole proving-ourselves cycle makes us feel small. It keeps us from living our lives fully and feeling like we matter. We were never meant to live our lives small or to hide in our lives. We were meant to live fully as ourselves. We learn smallness and hiding as we grow up.

I spent much of my life shrinking into myself so I could get the approval of others. I thought it was the only way to matter in the world, that it was the only way to convince people to want to be around me and to love me. This really is not the case. It may sound a bit harsh but if the people around you are not comfortable with you being 100% your authentic self, then are they the "right" people to be around? That may sound and feel scary. I get it. For a long time, I was terrified of being alone and I would let others take centre stage so they might, in appreciation, throw me a scrap of their love. It's no way to live. It's not how we are meant to live.

I fell into this trap. Yes, that is what I'm going to call it, a trap. I didn't start out as a sparkly little three-year-old trying to prove I mattered. I simply *did* matter. Me. One hundred percent. I learned otherwise along the way and fell into the trap of the proving cycle. The vicious thing about the proving cycle is that once you are in it, it is amazingly difficult to get out of. It's like a hamster wheel and just like the hamster, we run around and around. But we can also get tossed off the wheel, which is what happened to me when my former partner decided to leave me. Yep, the Universe had definitely wanted me to have a wakeup call because I was so far off my path I couldn't even see straight anymore.

Honestly, when things finally came to a head, I had no idea how far down the rabbit hole of proving myself I had travelled. That pattern of behaviour had become so ingrained in my daily life that I didn't notice it anymore. It was a part of me. Part of my routine, one might say. My go-to move was to believe that any negative things that happened were my fault and I spent endless moments apologizing for myself.

At times it felt like I was apologizing for my existence. Once you get into the apologizing mode that deeply it's hard to come out of it. It is still a challenge for me sometimes today. Sometimes I don't even realize I'm doing it. Recently as an action item from my business coach she asked me to stop apologizing and to start living everyday unapologetically. As a matter of fact, that has become one of the core items in the mission statement of my company: to live unapologetically, to operate unapologetically, and to assist my clients to step into their lives more unapologetically. Life is not supposed to be lived in a constant state of apology. We are meant to thrive, be seen, and heard.

Even now, with all the powerful work I have undertaken to rise above my negative programming, I still sometimes have to remind myself that life is supposed to be joyous, and that being me, and living from my authentic heart, is my most precious gift. It's a gift to be treasured, used wisely, and shared. When you have spent decades trying to prove yourself it takes a bit of time to write a new story and not allow the old one to seep back in. As I've mentioned, there is a season for everything, and it is no different for the stories we have embedded deep within; their truth feels tangible! It can feel scary to let them go and step into something else.

The reward is immense when you make the choice to do so. When you are proving that you matter in various aspects of your life what you are saying nonverbally is that you don't matter. This belief subconsciously sneaks into your speech patterns and the words you use. It sneaks into your posture. You sit as far back into your chair as possible so you can be part of the conversation but set apart. This belief shows itself displayed loudly in the bathroom mirror as you do your hair or brush your teeth.

My inner chatter would remind me how unaverage I was and who was I kidding by putting on makeup as though I were as pretty as other women. It affects your decision-making. Making decisions was a brutal process: I wanted them to be right and show I knew what I was doing but I doubted myself continuously. Even alone time with my thoughts was consumed with self-doubt. When I would read, if I couldn't get lost in the story fast enough my inner chatter would start going over everything I hadn't done right or wonder if I might have upset someone. When this happened, I would isolate myself from the person/people my mind told me I had offended. Even though no one had said anything directly to me. I would interpret their actions as anger toward me. It poisoned every minute of every day because I couldn't let my guard down.

I touched my toe onto the hamster wheel of proving when I was around seven years old. It sounds early, but I figured out I didn't fit in soon after I started school. I would do small things to prove myself. I would try to be friends with everyone, especially the kids in the "in group." If I could just be part of that group, then everyone else would like me and then I would be "golden"…I would matter. That didn't turn out to be the case. All it did was make me feel like I didn't measure up *even more*.

Children, especially little girls, can smell desperation on you and they reject it. So, of course, I couldn't get into the "in crowd" because I was too desperate. The ironic part was I actually did fit in with the "in crowd," but I just couldn't see it. Years later I talked with one of people who had been part of the "in crowd" and she said how she had admired how I had fit in with so many different groups at school. I was surprised at this because back in the day I was so blinded by trying to prove myself that I couldn't see what was in front of me. It made my childhood and teenage years more daunting than they needed to be, and things just got worse as I moved on into my 20s, 30s, and halfway through my 40s.

One might wonder why it took me so long to make the choice to stop proving myself. Well, as I said, it was a well-practiced habit, and my environment supported that behaviour. After all, I was the conductor of my own orchestra. I had taught everyone around me really well how to treat me. When you hesitate too much to make a decision all the time because you are trying to make the exact right choice that will suit everyone, it looks like you can't make a decision at all. So, other people take over. When you sit back and let others do all the talking in a conversation, you get left out of the conversation, and it feels like your opinion matters less. It doesn't really, but it feels that way and you withdraw more instead of taking a stand for yourself and your opinion. Taking a stand is scary because it rocks the boat and you're not sure if you might get tossed out. Better to play it safe.

Where Has Playing Safe Gotten You?

I would ask you though…where has playing it safe gotten you? Are you loving the life of playing it safe? Are you living the life you want or deserve? Ah…there is that word again: deserve. To me the word "deserve" goes along with this whole conversation because when you are in the cycle of proving and mattering you don't feel like you deserve anything. You are grateful for what comes your way as you have conditioned yourself to be okay with that and you accept it. I remember purchasing a home and thinking, "it's nice, I really like it," but the thought underneath the idea was, "this is as good as I will ever get." I didn't think I deserved anything more. Again, that wasn't the reality at all and none of this really had anything to do with the house. It had more to do with what my heart was telling me about my life.

Eventually my heart started to whisper that I deserved to be happy. That there *was* more to me than I was allowing. That I had a choice. I hadn't realized I had a choice about how my life was supposed to go and that I could create my future. I thought in those days that life happens *to* us and that somehow, I was getting what I deserved. It was hard to reconcile. And I couldn't for a very long time.

As I said, I got tossed off the hamster wheel and what a relief because my partner's decision to leave me was what I needed to trigger me into starting to live my life. It was a journey, but it was the opening to shining my light and allowing myself to live as me without proving, protecting, or trying to matter.

Can you imagine what happened? My life turned around. I started talking and living. I started being part of the conversation instead of being a mouse in the background waiting for an opening to grab a scrap. The most important thing that happened was with each step my understanding grew…I did matter, and I always had.

I sincerely hope that by reading this book you can jump off that hamster wheel yourself at a much earlier stage of life. It takes a bit of courage, but I know you have it in you. When you practice something for that long it is like that old sweater in the back of your closet that you just don't get around to throwing out, even though you know you should.

Enriching My Life

Now I do things that make my heart sing, and I don't apologize for them. I go on trips and experience the world. I've met many wonderful people in my travels and on this journey, for which I am grateful. All of them have enriched my life in one way or another. Funny, the house I have now is similar in size to the one I mentioned earlier but it feels different because it feels like a home. It is somewhere I chose because it made me happy. My words when I stood in the kitchen for the first time were "I'm home." It makes all the difference in the world when you live life from your heart and allow joy and happiness to be your overarching choice points. When you allow *you* out into the world, life changes from being a struggle, to being wonderful.

It takes work and it takes opening up to others and not being alone. It also takes allowing the world to see your vulnerable side. In proving yourself, you have learned to not let anyone see your vulnerability. Squirrel it away so no one can use it against you. What I learned through opening up, reading a lot of books, investing in myself with mentors, and journalling like a mad fiend to get all the old ugly thoughts out of me, is that my thoughts changed and my journalling started to transform from "the ugly" to what I wanted my life to look like. Dreams started creeping in as well. As all of this happened, I started to shine my light out more and more into the world. As I did that and embraced myself more and more my vulnerability started to show as well because it is part of me and nothing to be ashamed of.

As an exercise to assist you to open to be more vulnerable, more yourself out in the world, start with journalling. No one has to see it and you can burn it later if you choose. I still have many of my journals and I look back from time to time to remind myself how far I have come. So, grab a journal and your pen and start by writing…

What would it look like if I allowed myself to shine out into the world?

Let all your thoughts roll out onto the page. Next write…

What would it look like if I allowed others to see my vulnerable side as I stood strong as me in the world?

Let you your thoughts roll onto the page. Don't censor anything, just let it roll. Next write…

What would it cost me to be vulnerable and be me?

Again, you know what I'm going to say: just let it flow. Finally, I invite you to write…

What would my life look like if I were to stand strong and go after the life I deserve? What dreams would I follow?

When you journal in this way, you relinquish the control you have been exerting over all aspects of your life. You can breathe more deeply and live more fully. When I did this my thoughts shifted from being consumed with mattering to being filled with hopes and dreams. My health dramatically improved and continues to improve today as I embrace myself more and more. I've learned to live life and instead of it being a daily struggle, it's a journey of adventure that is full of learning and understanding.

Doesn't that sound more appealing? More exciting? I'll give you an example of what this looked like. Back in the day, I would get up early in the morning and get ready for work. I would agonize in the bathroom to try and make myself look presentable. I never felt I succeeded in that regard because I didn't think the person looking back at me from the mirror was very pretty. The clothes I put on had one function: to hide my body. That was another aspect to how I thought I didn't measure up. I would then hop in my car and drive to work. As I mentioned earlier, it was a job I liked in the beginning but soon it became nothing more than a way to pay the bills. The workplace became a toxic environment and I had to leave. I didn't leave, however, until it was so painful it was affecting my life. I found another job and it was literally out of the frying pan and into the fire. Another job that wasn't for me. I was proving myself so hard in that job—it was awful.

That contrasts with my life today. Now I wake up with energy and greet my day with an adventurous attitude. Before I hop out of bed, I think of several "I am grateful for" statements. Then my feet hit the floor and my day starts. The mirror is now not a horrible thing to look in as I get ready for my day. I like the woman looking back at me. My clothes are no longer something to hide my body, but they are rather an expression of me. My workday now is enjoyable because I work with people I want to work with. Most days are magical as I now see the beauty surrounding me. I get to use my creative abilities in my work. I have the most amazing conversations. And the most spectacular part is that I no longer try to prove myself. I am who I am, and I've learned to love myself and let others see me.

Angela's Design Keys to Living Out

Key #6
You have always mattered. It's time to start believing it and living it. Proving you matter was never your job in the first place and it's time to move onto your real job, living the life you deserve.

For my personal message
Scan the QR Code with your smart phone
Or go to: https://youtu.be/OVcL0sCnaXU

Chapter Seven

Inner Chatter is Debilitating!

Inner Chatter: the voice inside your head that can take you from looking in the mirror to sobbing on the bathroom floor in under 30 seconds.
—Angela Wilson

About five years ago I flew to Costa Rica for a group retreat. I was looking forward to the trip, but I had some trepidation as I knew I was going to be with a group of people I couldn't hide from, and we would be continuing our exploration of "remembering" who we are. This wasn't my first retreat and wouldn't be my last but on the way to this particular one my inner chatter decided to do a number on me. It started at the airport. I bumped into one of the people who was going to the same retreat.

I was pleased, as I had developed a real bond with her over the years and seeing her quieted my nerves a bit. Jeannie gave me a big hug as she always does, and we sat beside each other to talk. She took a selfie of us—one that has come to be one of my favourite pictures of the two of us. But that day my inner chatter started. "Oh my god, look at how big you are!" I set it aside and we talked until our plane boarded.

I was alone with my mind for the next three hours until I reached the connecting airport. I managed to push my mind chatter aside several times and focus elsewhere. I completed the short layover and boarded my next flight, without Jeannie this time. I went to fasten my seat belt and it wouldn't fit. "OMG, why is this happening to me? OMG, I'm going to have to ask for a seat belt extender. Oh F#@k, everyone is going to know how truly fat I am."

I got the attention of the flight attendant and asked for the extender. She was lovely and discreet, but the damage was done. Now I had about four hours to let my negative thoughts rumble around. I did my very best to work my way out of the funk I was in and by the time my flight landed, and I met up with a couple of others who were on the retreat, I had managed to stuff it down. When you try to stuff this type of thing down, though, it erupts like a volcano later when you least expect it.

We had fun sightseeing for the rest of the day and evening and I was able to keep my thoughts somewhat at bay, but they were working in the background. The following day we met up with everyone else at the retreat location. That night my own personal Mount Vesuvius erupted. The group and a coach were all sitting around discussing our lives when out of nowhere, part of the bottom of the couch four of us were sitting on broke. I melted into a pile of tears on the floor because, clearly, it had broken because I was too fat. The tears were ferocious and overwhelming, and I couldn't do anything but let them out. The discussion changed to me and my reaction. I learned I had been so good at beating myself up for so long, and I had been stuffing my feelings and my emotions down so well, that I had hit a breaking point.

The Universe had orchestrated the timing perfectly, because I was with a group of people with whom I could be myself and they saw and knew the real me. I shared with the group the events that had transpired from the airport all the way up until that moment, even though I was embarrassed inside, and I was trembling like a leaf. But I did it. I knew in that moment I wanted to change the way I felt, and I wanted to move forward. Of course, throughout the conversation my friends kept pointing out to me the fact that I was not the only one on the couch.

I'd like to point out to you that throughout my life I have struggled with my size. I have always been tall, as I mentioned, with which comes a different bone structure. The teasing about my size that I experienced growing up stuck with me my whole life. In university, I got into a cycle of dieting and really slimmed down. Funny, I remember I received attention and comments when I was at my smallest. It added to my inner chatter of, "see, when you are small you get noticed, and people like you, so you better stay small." Unfortunately, as the years progressed, and I spiralled increasingly into an emotional pit, I kept gaining more weight. I would yell at myself for being fat and I would try to change but I did not have the ability to make the choices and take the steps to change.

When I was tossed off the hamster wheel when my former partner left, my weight dropped like a stone. Some of it crept back on because how I lost it (by not eating) was not sustainable or healthy. Today I will admit that my weight is still not where I would prefer it from a health standpoint, but I no longer beat myself up over it. As I mentioned, I like the woman staring back from me in the mirror. I'm now taking action to improve my health even further because I enjoy being active and being adventurous. It makes me happy because I love enjoying my life.

The Impact of Our Inner Chatter

So, there's the impact our inner chatter can have on us. Bear in mind that when I was immersed in the chatter I really couldn't see or think straight. It was like the inner chatter took me over and my rational mind went out the window. You know what else went out the window? The whispers from my heart. Those whispers couldn't possibility be heard because of the deafening volume of my inner chatter. If you would like to deal more powerfully with your own inner chatter, I invite you to find a touchstone moment from your past—a time when you were fully "you"—and think about how you felt. Remember the experience in vivid detail so you can go back there in a second. I find this is a good tool to presence myself to the "right now" moment. It snaps me out of my inner chatter loop. Quite often I end up smiling and saying, "damn, that took courage…I can do this."

To find this touchstone, take a seat and quiet your mind. Now, breathe deeply in and out six times. Let everything else drift away. Now think of a time when your heart was super full, and life was joyous. Stay with that feeling. And try to visualize the experience, this time more deeply. Can you see or sense your surroundings? Can you hear or sense any sounds? Can you smell or sense any smells? Are there any colours associated with what you are experiencing? Make this all as vivid as you can.

Ah… now you have it. Take in six more deep breaths while you are in this space. Now open your eyes and journal everything that came into your vision. When you do these two actions the experience becomes more real. Save what you write somewhere so you can go back to it. When your inner chatter amps up, pull it out and reread it. Then close your eyes and take six deep breaths and let the vision ripple through you. Your mind will shift, and your inner chatter will weaken. The other thing that will happen is that your mood will shift as well, and you will feel lighter and more like you.

Let's take a closer look at this topic of "Inner Chatter." You may have a different name for this voice. Some call it your "ego voice." Regardless of what we call it, this voice can seem terrifyingly real for many years. Even now my Inner Chatter can still take a bit of a toll on me—and even produce tears—but I've learned through my journey that I have the choice to listen to it or not and I can also choose to change its volume.

These are priceless tools.

So, what is it, exactly?

Here's how I define it: Inner Chatter is the voice inside your head that expresses your thoughts. It's almost like it's separate from you… but it isn't. I call it inner chatter to remind myself it is part of me and as such I have control over it. Typically, when it's going full steam ahead, our inner chatter is quite loud and quite believable. It doesn't become outrageous overnight but if you let it run amuck it can be quite destructive. Its tone is loud. Its words are negative. Its impact can be catastrophic. Its power is persuasive. It can be unrelenting.

Why do you think we let a voice like this exist within us? Wouldn't we just choose to think differently? Of course, we would, but that inner chatter is insidious, and it lurks in the shadows to jump out at us during our most vulnerable moments—you know, those moments when we are struggling with who we are.

My inner chatter built up steam and strength over time. It went hand in hand with all the other things we have been discussing because it was the voice inside me that reinforced everything I heard. It was a constant reminder of how truly small and unworthy I was. At its height, it could literally sink me into a sobbing pile on the bathroom floor in seconds. Because when I would look in the mirror to get ready for work, clean my teeth, wash my hands, whatever, it would use its "negative speak" on me.

This happened repeatedly. Picture if you can a woman standing looking in the bathroom mirror getting ready for work. She is doing her hair and her makeup and getting ready to greet the day. Initially, she thinks, "I look pretty good today."

Next, she reaches for something and catches a different angle of herself in the mirror. Her thought shifts instantly to, "Ohmygod I think this outfit might not fit right, oh no, is it too snug to wear out in public?"

Next thought: "How did you let yourself get so fat?"

Next: "Ohmygod I am so fat and ugly."

"Nobody could ever truly love someone like me."

At this point the voice amps up and the final blow to the floor is…"Why are you kidding yourself? You are fat, ugly, and worth-less." Sometimes worth-less changed to "stupid," "a fraud," etc., depending on what was going on at the time.

That was my inner chatter, hard at work, and although what triggered it for me was typically my size, you may have other issues that send your inner chatter into overdrive. At this point, you may be wondering why I'm describing it as though it were a separate entity. That's because in the beginning, it felt like it actually *was* a separate entity. I knew the words were in my own head so they couldn't be separate from me, but it sure felt that way. When I think now about the words I used on myself I can see that they were just horrible. I would never have talked to anyone else in that manner. That voice is powerful and can create powerful outcomes.

Here's another example of an inner chatter experience that has had a strong *positive* impact on my life:

Travelling to Tanzania

I had joined the Toronto Camera Club and was excited about their upcoming group trip to Tanzania. Going to the Serengeti was a dream of mine so when the opportunity came up, I jumped at it.

At one of the meetings prior to our departure we discussed ideal camera equipment. I listened to the recommendations and tried to keep myself from falling out of my chair onto the floor.

They were recommending three cameras, but I didn't have that type of equipment yet! I had found the joy of photography, but my inner chatter kept reminding me that I wasn't very good and that these people knew more and were more talented. I drove home from the meeting and called my sister in tears. When I explained how inadequately prepared I felt, and wondered how I could possibly think I could pull this off, she stopped me and said, "Of *course* you have three cameras. You have your DSLR, you have your point and shoot, and you have your phone." Simple fix, done, it was figured out.

Soon thereafter I met the love of my life. We talked a lot about the trip, and I remember that just before I left, he asked what animal I wanted to see the most. I remember saying, "whichever ones we see will be great, but I can't wait to see the vastness of the Serengeti." The day came to leave, and I was off to the airport. I got there and all of a sudden, my inner chatter started up fast and furious, to the point where I couldn't even remember what anyone I was going to be travelling with looked like. That revved up my anxiety even more. I texted my new-found love and he was so supportive; he reminded me everything was going to be okay. Sure enough, once at my gate, I recognized some of the people from the club.

Next, my inner chatter started at me because I was listening to all the accomplishments the photographers were talking about and, again, I received reassuring texts from Gord. Those texts allowed me to breathe and refocus.

I boarded the plane and had the trip of a lifetime. I discovered a lot about myself on the Serengeti and I discovered I had the exact right amount of camera equipment. Honestly, Tanzania was one of the turning points of my life because I went with a group of 14 people who I didn't know at all. I remember our main tour guide, Ryan, asking me the first night we were in the mobile tent camp if it was the accommodations that had made me so nervous about coming on the trip.

My response was, "absolutely not. It was the fact that I didn't know anyone." This was one of the best experiences of my life. It completely opened my heart and reminded me of the courage I do have inside. When I'm unsure about anything in life, I remember back to that trip and the vastness of the Serengeti.

We learn from our experiences. I have also come to listen to the words my inner chatter is using and when they become negative in nature, or too loud, I make the choice to shift my thoughts and change the words. I've learned over time that my inner chatter is actually my inner bully. The hurtful, angry, words I used on myself would be used by a bully on someone else. They were not words that a friend would use on a friend. Once I gained more discernment, I realized I had the ability to choose whether to listen or not. I also learned I could turn down the volume. And just like a bully, when you stand up and say, "not this time," they turn and go, because you have not allowed their power to supersede yours.

I'm not saying that figuring out how to deal with your inner chatter is an easy task, because it's not. I'm also not going to tell you that it will completely go away because I don't think it does. But I do know that with time you learn to use it to assist you in understanding when you are out of alignment with your authentic self. One of the ways I do this is by going through the following process as I journal.

Be open to what comes.

Take an inner chatter thought, don't engage in it, and write it down.

Look at what is behind the thought.
What is the feeling?

What do you think this looks like?

If this is true, what does it bring up?

Is there evidence in your life to show that it isn't true? Give examples.

With evidence that the inner chatter is false, then what is true?

Let your mind just be quiet and let your heart voice (inner knowing) talk to you because it will show you the way.

For more details regarding this process go to my website www.angelaunlimited.com. You can download a free PDF that gives you more details and an example.

To hear your inner knowing you need to quiet your mind. Your inner chatter (ego brain) filters everything and uses past events as reference points; it rarely chooses the good ones. It chooses struggle to keep you stuck. Your inner knowing pulls you forward and guides you to shine your light and be abundant.

It takes courage to tackle your inner chatter just like it takes courage to stand up to any other bully. But here is what I know as the truth of you: you have that courage within, even if you might not quite know it yet. I imagine you've had glimpses of it, like I did, when my inner knowing kept reminding me there was more available to me. The other thing I know is this: you are worth the effort it takes to stand up to your inner bully and inner chatter. You deserve to shine your light and not hide in its shadow.

Angela's Design Keys to Living Out Loud

Key #7

Even when it doesn't feel like it, you have control over your inner chatter. You have the choice to listen or not. You also have the choice to turn the volume down. Stand up courageously to this bully and listen to your inner knowing instead.

For my personal message
Scan the QR Code with your smart phone
Or go to: https://youtu.be/9AO-6QVdej4

Chapter Eight

Emotions Guide Us

Emotions are our guiding light. When we squash them down, we are squashing our light. The more we do this the more we lose ourselves.
—Angela Wilson

Early in my career I worked for a big accounting firm where I had a female manager. I went to her one day because I was overwhelmed by the amount of work assigned to me and I had some personal issues to deal with all at the same time. She closed her door and talked kindly to me about the situation, and I ended up in tears. Nothing more was said at that point, so I thought, "okay that was behind closed doors, and it happened just once." Unfortunately, that was not the end of it. In my performance evaluation she mentioned that I needed to improve my demeanour at work as crying was not an acceptable response to workload issues. I was shocked and horrified but I learned that day to:

a) not trust and
b) never allow my emotions to show again, even behind closed doors when I thought it was safe, and
c) I was not safe.

What a set of lessons to learn early in a career! It stuck with me for a long time. I have rarely shown tears in a work setting since that time. And every single time they have later been used as a weapon against me. This of course added to my fear/safety issues, my inner chatter, my self-worth issues, and my protective layers. It takes a lot of layers to suck up tears. So, understandably, I thought emotions were a bad thing. Plus, when they finally did erupt it was like an explosion. I didn't know how to deal with them. I didn't know when or where they were appropriate, if at all. How do you navigate through those waters?!

Emotions are like gatekeepers that let us know if we are in congruence with ourselves or not. I haven't until recently had a very good relationship with my emotions. I learned very young that emotions were not a positive thing at all, and it was best to stuff them down, but I never understood why.

Excitement and pure joy were fine, but anger and sadness were not. And if they did come out, they should be tucked away quickly. Don't get me wrong I laughed and played, which was perfectly fine, but I was taught that I shouldn't be too loud, so I didn't disturb others. It always felt like we were all supposed to hover at the middle of the road. The same rules resonated through the hallways of my school, except that the acceptable band of emotions was narrower. Anger and sadness were not allowed, and joyfulness had to be expressed in a respectful manner. Again, we were all supposed to conform to the social setting. No one ever explained what emotions were or why we had them. They were just an unacceptable part of being a little girl.

I remember watching how different people reacted to different emotions and how some used their emotions to get praise or comforting, or other things they wanted. I remember one time trying this theory out at a testing day for figure skating in my early teens. I was testing for two different levels that day, and the results came up fairly quickly. I hadn't passed my dance test to move forward so

I decided to cry to get a reaction from my dad. It didn't work. I was told to stop it and behave myself. I was being foolish. This confirmed for me that I shouldn't try that again, and also that showing tears in public was not okay. Dad's voice was not harsh or threatening, just steady and matter of fact.

As a teenager, I also learned that girls shouldn't show emotion because they labelled us. If we were too happy all the time, we were called a Pollyanna, or thought to have our heads in the clouds. If we were angry, then there was something wrong with us because young women were not supposed to be angry unless there was an extreme reason and even then, our anger should dissipate quickly. And tears? Well, they were a whole other ball game because if you cried you were labelled a hysterical female and/or you were considered weak. Polite young ladies did not cry in public. If we did start to cry, we had to get to the bathroom quickly, out of sight, and dry those tears. What an exhausting way to live.

Being Vulnerable in the Workplace

It's fascinating, though, because when we grew up to become part of the professional workforce women were also penalized for showing emotion. I think the workplace is changing a bit as people realize being vulnerable in an authentic way is healthy and quite courageous. But we still struggle with mixed messages: for the most part a strong tough female boss is thought of as a "bitch" whereas a man is confident and just doing his job.

I've learned since those years that emotions are a very valuable tool. They tell us when we are or are not aligned. It's magical. It took time to learn this. As I started to explore the idea that emotions are not wrong, and that they are a tool for understanding ourselves, my emotions would splatter all over the map. You know, it's like the little kid who isn't allowed to eat sweets and then they get the opportunity to have a cookie. Well, they don't eat one cookie. They eat the plateful, or the entire bag of cookies, because they are so good, and they know they are forbidden. What that kid doesn't know is that they are yummy going down but later their stomach is not going to be happy. Taking the flood gates off of a lifetime of stuffing down your emotions creates a similar situation. It's like the dam opens and you get washed down the river for a while. But you do find your footing and you do learn the direction you are being pointed in.

Remember that trip I took to Costa Rica? That's when I really started to understand what my emotions were trying to convey to me. I shed a lot of tears on that trip. It felt like every time I turned around, I was crying. Then the trip facilitator did an exercise with me. She asked me what the smell of being upset was. At first, I thought *"what the hell are you talking about?"* but I continued to listen to what she was saying. I realized at the moment there was an "off" smell, a rotten smell.

I learned through the exercise that when I had tears and I noticed that smell, then what I was upset about was not the truth. It was "off," or rotten. We actually laughed and started calling it the sniff test. I used that exercise for quite some time. Now what I do is look at the intensity behind the emotion. If I'm angry or sad and it is a super intense feeling, I know that the object of that anger or sadness is not the truth. It is something my ego and inner chatter are making up and I let it go. I still at times get angry and I get sad but now I can measure those emotions. Now when they come up, I don't act on them. I let them sit and see what they are about. Sometimes they are showing me how I've been judgemental about someone or something, or where I have been out of my integrity.

When we are out of our integrity it means we are not aligned with ourselves, and we are not listening to our inner knowing. We are coming at everything from our thinking brain instead of from our heart. When we are in that space, we can become very judgemental of others and ourselves. This leads to negative mind speak and it gives our inner chatter more space to play, which is never good. We can't be our true, authentic selves when we are in this mindset. And it causes us to start feeling bad and retreat further into the shadows.

Working with Our Emotions

When we learn how to work with our emotions and understand them, they can be such a precious guide. Have you ever felt so peaceful that you can feel there are thousands of possibilities floating around for you? This is when you are centred and grounded in your knowing. This is the state where, if you are open to life's magic, it happens. Have you ever been angry at a situation and when you actually notice your inner chatter you realize that the statements your egoic mind are making are all righteous and indignant and totally blaming another person or situation? Well, that's your guidance telling you that you are not in your truth and that the situation you are dwelling on is not the truth. I've also learned, at times when I feel a sense of sadness, to let it sit. Because this sometimes happens when an old pattern is coming up and the protective layer it is wrapped in is decaying. Those feelings of sadness are usually followed by a profound sense of peaceful calmness.

As you can see, your relationship with your emotional world is very powerful and it is important to embrace it, work with it, and learn from it. Your emotions are not bad, or evil, or wrong. They are part of your guidance system. And as part of your guidance system, they are unique to you. Mine guide me back to a place of knowing and integrity. When I'm operating completely from my authentic heart, I am peaceful and joyful. I have energy, and I feel like I can conquer the world. I can see my dreams before my eyes. It's magical. When I'm misaligned, sadness, anger, and doubt set in. When those show up, I know to be gentle with myself and to have grace so I can hear my knowing and get back into my authentic heart. When I first started understanding my relationship with my emotions, this would take a long time. Now it doesn't because I know that once I can see the shadow of the misalignment, my light can bust through it.

I would like to give you an exercise to gauge your emotions and learn how to view their message to you. First, when emotion comes up, how does it feel to you? Let's do this exercise with a perceived negative emotion such as sadness. When you feel sad do you let it take you over? If yes, what are the words you are using in your mind? Write them down. Take those words and change them to positive words because the ones you are using when sadness takes you over will be negative in nature.

By changing our thoughts, we can reduce the hold sadness has on us. Is the sadness still there and still quite acute? If yes, then ask yourself if this sadness is even yours. Sometimes we pick up on other people's sadness or allow ourselves to become affected by other circumstances which make us sad. If the sadness is not yours, take a few deep breaths for at least a minute and let it release out as though you were setting it free from you.

If it is yours, sit with it and see what is behind it. Are you feeling hurt or betrayed, for example? If so, what is there for you to do? Journalling and letting the words and feelings roll out onto the page works for me at times like this. Don't censor your words, just let them roll out of you freely on the page. What I experience is a dissipation in intensity as the thoughts fly onto the page. This is a practice and there is no right or wrong. Don't analyze the words and feelings as they roll out of you. Analyzing keeps us in the spot of feeling the emotion and engaging in the thoughts that brought us to this space in the first place. Feel the feels, let them roll through, and set them free.

We all have the ability to learn and understand our emotions. Your experience of this will be different from mine because we are all unique and so our emotional guidance is unique as well. There is no cookie-cutter way to become fluent with our emotions and what they tell us, but if you choose to embark on the journey of understanding what yours are telling you, I can tell you there are great rewards along the way. I went from stuffing every emotion down into the depths of the well of me, to seeing them erupt uncontrollably all over the place, to thinking maybe there was something wrong with me, to learning it was all okay, to now knowing my emotions are here to guide me.

As with everything else in life and in this book, this, too, is a learning experience. It is part of your journey, and you get to choose what parts you want to lean into and understand and what parts you want to leave as is for the moment. Unpacking and understanding how your emotions guide you can be scary, but I have no doubt you have the courage to do so. Remember: we aren't sprinting to a finish line we are having the adventure of a lifetime. So, why not embrace all the guidance and tools we can, to make it the most kick-ass journey ever?!

Angela's Design Keys to Living Out Loud

Key #8
Emotions are part of our guidance system. Embracing them and learning how they guide us is one of the best ways to live while shining our light out into the world.

For my personal message
Scan the QR Code with your smart phone
Or go to: https://youtu.be/zeV9JCkUT-o

Chapter Nine

Living in the Shadow of Shame

*Living in the shadows of shame means we are
living as a morphed version of ourselves
instead of the best version of ourselves.*
—Angela Wilson

Shame used to be part of every aspect of my life. I felt ashamed because of my size. I felt ashamed because I wasn't as smart as other people. I felt ashamed because I couldn't seem to measure up. I felt ashamed around the ending of my relationship. But none of that shame was truly mine because it wasn't who I am in my heart. My heart wasn't ashamed. It was my ego that took on the task of telling me all the things I should be ashamed of, and my inner chatter amplified everything.

Have you ever felt ashamed of who you are? It is a lonely feeling, and very powerful. It led me to dark thoughts and a habit of isolating myself because I didn't want to admit how I felt to anybody, even myself. The shame added more protective layers around me, and it tightened the weave of the fabric of the ones that were already holding me in their grip.

Shame is a huge topic, and many people study it. One of the leading shame experts is researcher and storyteller Brené Brown. She has studied this subject extensively and written many books about it. I quite like a quote from her book *I Thought it Was Just Me (but it isn't)*:

> *"When we find the courage to share our experiences and the compassion to hear others tell their stories we force shame out of hiding and end the silence."*[3]

This quote is a reminder that it takes courage to speak our truth and allow our voices to be heard in the world, just like I'm doing with this book. This book is a way for me to use my voice, to assist others who may have had or are having experiences which my insights can illuminate. I talk about shadows a lot because I feel that if we are not being our true selves and putting the best possible version of ourselves out into the world, then we are living in the shadows. No one benefits when we are living in the shadows. Not us, and not the world. We are not here to be small in our journey. We are here to be on the full adventure of being us. Shame puts the brakes on that adventurous journey.

Shame also keeps us in a perpetual space of smallness, and the fear that surrounds it feels almost tangible. Living in the world of "Unworthy and Inadequate" increases your fear of allowing yourself to be seen. It increases your fear of using your voice. It ramps up your inner chatter; it is utterly brutal. At least this is what happened to me. If you can identify with this, I'm sorry. No one, and I mean no one, should have to feel that way.

Is shame holding you in the shadows? It held me there for many years in a lot of situations and I had to really work hard at not allowing it

---

[3] Brown, Brené, *I Thought It Was Just Me (But it Wasn't)*, Avery, New York, pg 127.

to control me anymore. We must be vigilant against engaging in the shadow of shame. If we buy into every societal construct we will feel a great deal of shame…daily. When we do this, we live by ideas others have created that somehow became acceptable in society and these may not be our ideas at all. For example, you might feel embarrassed or ashamed after a divorce because that isn't something that is prevalent in your social or family circle. Or you could feel shame around money because your family or friends judge people who are financially successful. The result? You downplay your achievements.

Shame showed up many times and in many ways in my life. I was in such turmoil on the inside. I had a great yearning to be me, but I felt completely worth-less and inadequate. At that time, a wonderful person I knew shared with me her view that I was keeping myself small and that we are not meant to play small in our lives. I thought about this and started to take miniscule steps toward opening up, trying to find my confidence, and expressing myself more. It was around this time the relationship I mentioned ended.

At first, I blamed myself for being so foolish as to try and use my voice. This had to be my fault somehow. I felt shame around trying to improve myself and shame at not being able to make my relationship succeed. These shames don't walk with me today and every time my confidence wavers, I remind myself we are not meant to be small. We are meant to live fully as ourselves.

Every one of us has a great deal of magnificence inside and we are each meant to express all of it…but we play small because we have learned to be ashamed of who we are, or the circumstances we live in. I hope as you are reading this you are getting a sense that there is another way of being. The shadow of shame that perpetuates your feeling of smallness, worth-lessness, and inadequacy can be busted apart. It takes courage. It takes listening to your heart and not your head. It takes choosing to say, "Yes, there is more to me than this and I'm going on the journey of my lifetime."

Small-Dose Shame

Shame can come in small doses or large ones. The small ones are what I call everyday ongoing societal doses. For me the daily shame was about not measuring up and it manifested itself in several ways, particularly with regard to my size. You see, the more I went down the wormhole of being ashamed of who I was the more my weight increased. And the more weight I put on the more I beat myself up and verbally abused myself with my inner chatter. With that cycle playing I became even more ashamed of my appearance, and I sunk deeper into feeling worth-less and unlovable.

After all, in my head I was this large grotesque creature—and how could anyone love that? Shame about my physical appearance shadowed every look I took in the mirror. I was viewing myself through a distorted lens. I was so concerned that everyone just viewed me as someone who was fat and didn't care anymore that I tried to wear clothing that gave the appearance I was striving to change my physical self. I would wear pants with a long baggy top open over another top. I always made sure I wore great shoes so my ensemble would seem more fashionable. Everything I wore represented an attempt to hide my body, but I always added in splashes of colour because in my mind that meant I hadn't given up. I was still trying.

The small-dose shame creeps in and compounds. You may not even see it until the shadow is well cast but it can be enormously detrimental. We often don't really see it until we are securely rooted in it. Have you ever felt like this or something similar? Well, one thing I do know is that there is a way out the other side.

Large-Dose Shame

The large-dose shames are the big ones that show up at a single point in time. The ending of my relationship came out of the blue and I was devastated. I remember feeling many shards of shame. I was the only one in my family who had ever experienced the stain of the demise of a relationship. I couldn't believe I had been unable to make things work. I thought, "*What a failure. What an idiot. I'm worth-less.*" I spent the first few months after the split hardly talking to anyone. As time went on and the shame cloud started to lift, I opened myself to more and more people. As the shame lifted so did my hopes that I would meet someone else. Even through the shame I could get a glimpse in my heart that I was loveable. Maybe I just needed to be patient.

Large-dose shames do seem to dissipate because they are derived from an event or specific point in time and, therefore, they are less anchored into our sense of who we are. I allowed myself to become more open and I started expressing myself. Eventually, I met a wonderful man who I knew in a short period of time was my soul mate, my partner in everything. That man became my husband, and I am grateful every day that he came into my life.

We can move past shame if we choose to do so, as I did following my large-dose example of it. I have progressed through the small doses of shame as well, but they take a little more time and it's been my experience that we must be vigilant to keep those smaller shames at bay. This is a marathon, not a sprint, and shames that have been embedded deeply and repeatedly over many years sometimes pop back up when we least expect them. I do think it is important to choose to move past our shame because it takes such a toll on us physically, mentally, emotionally, and spiritually.

It's interesting that after my relationship ended my weight dropped quickly and dramatically. When it levelled off people couldn't believe how much I had lost. I remember feeling good and feeling good *in my body* at that time, although the reality was, I had been in such turmoil that I couldn't eat. The shame of not being in a relationship anymore, and of not being loved, took my appetite away. It came back somewhere around the time I released the shame that surrounded that phase of my life.

For years now I have been on the journey of figuring out a better way of being in tune with my body and listening to what it is telling me. It takes time to remember how to listen to your body and understand that it is giving us clues all the time about what it needs and requires. My shroud of shame made me forget how to pay attention and treat my body with kindness.

Even after I had begun to embrace a more loving way of being with myself, I continued to wonder what was wrong: "*I'm happy now,*" I thought. "*Why isn't my body responding the way I want it to?*" I thought when I was happy that my body would feel vibrant, stay lean, and it would settle to a pleasant calmness. Well, what I've learned—with the help of a few loving souls—is that when you spend as much time as I did on "high alert" it takes time for things to settle to a new normal. I had trained my inner chatter to tell me what it thinks is best, at the expense of what my body was telling me. I had to train myself to listen to my body, again, too.

All of this is part of the magnificent journey of life and without these experiences I wouldn't be enjoying the amazing journey of being me. I would be existing as a distorted version of me. This adventurous journey of life requires us to stand in our courageous hearts as there are diversions along the way. One of those diversions is shame. We have a choice, though, to stand in the shadow of shame or to step away from it. What would your life look like right now if you took one small step away from the shadow of shame? Stepping away from my own shadow of shame was freeing, and my life changed on all levels. There are a lot of shame points built into our society. No one tells us that we get to choose to allow them in or not. Instead, we learn to get bogged down in the same old stories swirling around us. To live as the best version of ourselves we need to step beyond the same game and be all of who we are meant to be. I know it will be scary at first but in my experience, it is really worth the effort.

An exercise to assist you with moving away from shame and living the life you deserve is to stop when you are feeling shame and ask yourself what is causing me to feel shame. Is it inside me or outside of me? If it is outside, think of how you can set it aside and not allow it to affect you so much. Look at it and ask yourself if this will matter in a year. Will it matter in two years? What about in five years? If the answer is, "no," or, "probably not," then I encourage you to take six deep breaths and make a choice to take one small step to move away from the issue.

If it is inside you, ask yourself, "what am I getting out of feeling this shame? What would be different if I just let it go?" Look at the thoughts that are surrounding it and shift the language you are using in your thoughts. When we are in the thought pattern of shame our thoughts tend to be negative and of a low vibration. Try turning them around so the words are more positive and uplifting. Once you have noticed this try choosing to take one action step to keep your thoughts positive. Don't analyze it too deeply as when we dwell on the issue, we can spiral down a huge rabbit hole which is hard to dig out of. Instead, recognize it and then make the choice to take an action step away from the shame.

An example of this would be each morning to look in the mirror and say today I want to take steps to live the life I deserve. I want joy and happiness in my life. Then as your day progresses look for evidence of this and look for the beauty around you. It is hard to live in shame when we are noticing the beauty and joy in life.

Let's bust through the shadow of shame and start breathing—and amplifying ourselves out into the world as the best version of ourselves we can possibly be. We were never meant to be small or to hide in the shadows of shame. We were meant to live our life fully as the divine children we came into this world to be. Our three-year-old selves knew life was unlimited and didn't know what shame was. We learned about it over time and just as we learned that, we can learn something else. I hope you choose to not let shame continue to rule and suffocate you.

Angela Design Keys to Living Out Loud

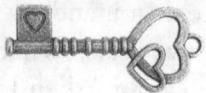

Key #9
Live as the best version of you and stand out in the light instead of in the shadow of doubt. Break free from what others think, or their judgements of you, and be you. The world needs you and your voice. You are loved and you are worthy.

For my personal message
Scan the QR Code with your smart phone
Or go to: https://youtu.be/SyxiydaN_qk

Chapter Ten

Hiding In Plain Sight

*Hiding in plain sight is a game that takes your
voice away. Using your voice and standing
fully in sight allows the magnificent you to shine.*
—Angela Wilson

Has someone ever made a comment to you that felt like a slap...but then they said, "I was only kidding," as a way to soften the sting, or to get back in your good books? Or have you ever been told you were too sensitive and that you take everything the wrong way? It drives us to hide, doesn't it?

The interesting aspect of hiding in plain sight is that it's a trick we play on ourselves. It really messes us up. It adds to our protective layer because being truly seen is one more thing we need to be on guard against. Being seen becomes another reason to beat ourselves up. Hiding becomes another huge blanket to wrap around ourselves. Because now, every time we are out somewhere, our guard has to be even higher, and we are more invested in keeping our true selves under wraps.

This ties in with losing our voice. I mentioned earlier that I could be in a crowd of people and not say a word. I was there, and everyone could see me, but I was hiding in plain sight. This reminds me of a conversation I had five years ago during the festivities celebrating my marriage to my current husband. Some of us decided to go fishing. While out on the boat one friend's husband asked me if I was okay because he said I was being much too quiet. When he said this, another friend's husband said, "Angela is normally quiet." The reply came back, "No, she isn't."

You see, both of these wonderful men had gotten to know me at different times in my life. The first one had gotten to know me in the past 10 years as I was remembering who I was and starting to use my voice. The second one knew me from my days of sitting back and allowing others to speak. It is rare now for me to be with a group of people and be silent. I mastered the art of hiding in plain sight over the course of a couple decades. This allowed me to function out in the world while hiding my thoughts, feelings, emotions, and my uniqueness inside protective invisible walls. I was—and still am—very social. I enjoy being around people, so people could always see the physical me, but no one saw the "real" me because I had her tied up inside me. People rarely caught a glimpse of her.

As I've mentioned, I pulled within because I couldn't handle the judgements and the opinions that swirled around me. My ears would take these comments in and then my inner chatter would repeat them again and again. I tried desperately to fix myself because clearly there was something wrong with me or people wouldn't say such mean things to me. I realize now that I wasted a huge amount of time trying to fix myself; I was never broken. I had just forgotten who I was at my heart because I had protected that aspect of me and hidden it away.

I also hid myself away by the way I dressed, choosing articles of clothing that hid as much of my physical body as possible. Nothing I owned accentuated my figure. By this time, I had a skewed view of the way I looked. If my partner and I went out for dinner, I would sometimes try to dress a little more sexily and put on some makeup, but I only did that when we would go to restaurants where the waitstaff and bartenders complimented—rather than judged—me. I would muster up my courage for a few hours and try to let a snippet of my true self be seen.

What I didn't realize at the time was that there were people who could see more of me than I realized, and I believe some of them worked in those restaurants. Of course, that courage would run away as before long at home my partner at the time would tell me I looked frumpy dumpy. I would try not to let it bother me, but it cut. I filtered what I heard through the lens of who I was at the time—this is still how it works today, but the lens is much different now. I'm sure my former partner would say that the meaning I put on the comments I heard was not what they intended and that I had heard it all wrong. But when we hear through our own ears, we are guided by all our past experiences.

Making Changes

It took courage, though, to stop hiding in this fashion. I worked at it little by little, the same way I had taken on that way of being in the first place. As I mentioned earlier, I lost a ton of weight. I had to buy new clothes and when I did, I would sometimes ask a friend for assistance. I think more often it was my friend instigating a shopping trip, as she would say, "Girl, we are going shopping because you need new clothes that fit!" It was a marvel to buy clothes that fit and receive compliments about my appearance. I didn't know how to take them, but they would come my way and helped me take little steps to remember me. All of me.

As I took more of these steps it became easier to be me, and to be actively involved in social situations. I realized that I used to use social settings to escape—to hide. I would fill my social calendar to the brim so when I was out somewhere, I could drift into the background. I could feel safe in my little hidey-hole even though I was surrounded by people. This was especially useful at times when my inner chatter was having one of its fabulous freak-outs. I could let the conversation go on while I dealt with what was going on inside. Unbeknownst to me at the time I was not always successful at this. Just a few years ago a friend mentioned how she had felt helpless because she could see me slipping further inside but she didn't know what to do.

She would try to get me on my own to have a conversation. She said that at first, she thought it worked a bit but after a while she noticed that even in those conversations I was withdrawn. When she told me this, I thanked her for being a good friend and for continuing to try. I told her she did the exact right thing—actually, the only thing she could do. She continued to reach out and she continued to try. I'm blessed to have such good friends in my life.

I no longer hide in social settings, and I no longer fill my social calendar with places to hide. Now I fill my time with wonderful friends with whom I want to have great conversations. I only sit back when I'm listening intently. Not all of our conversations are profoundly deep. Some of them are light-hearted and filled with laughter. I believe this is the way life is supposed to be: full of amazing conversations, laughter, and the company of people who have a kindred outlook. It is fascinating what we do to ourselves when we forget who we are, and we try to live up to what we perceive everyone else wants us to be. The turmoil and feelings of isolation it causes inside are unbelievable. I isolated myself internally even though I was out in the world working, entertaining, spending time with friends, and traveling. Like everything else, I did not become successful at hiding in plain sight overnight. It happened inch by inch, but it had a mountainous impact on me.

It took a huge amount of brain power to keep myself well-hidden and buttoned down. Functioning in the world was difficult. I felt I had to appear one way on the outside while I was screaming for freedom on the inside. My internal world became so daunting that I began losing my ability to contain it. It was bound to erupt and when it did, in response to the end of my relationship—the eruption was like nothing I had experienced in the past. I couldn't think straight or eat. I felt like out of the blue I had been hit up the side of my head with a two-by-four.

Early on I wondered how I could go on. I didn't trust myself and I was afraid to trust anyone else. I felt like my life was teetering on shaky ground. I remember one of my nieces telling me "Don't worry Auntie Angela you won't hit the bottom. We will catch you." That was one of several turning points for me. You see, I had always tried to be there for my nieces and nephews and then to have them support me was amazing. It was a sign to me that I did matter, and I was lovable.

I have learned that the world is a more beautiful place than I had ever imagined. I now look for beauty when I go for a walk, rather than just try to get somewhere. I engage in spectacular conversations, and I feel alive! I've also come to realize that I no longer have an option to hide because hiding does not serve me anymore. Am I uncomfortable at times? Yes, I am.

And some days I have to call on my courage to prevent the old patterns from slipping back in. When they appear, I recognize them for what they are, and from whence they sprang, and I allow them to move through me. Each time this happens, it becomes easier and the movement through me becomes faster. I now couldn't even imagine hiding in plain sight as I've become accustomed to living my life as the person, I am here to be; going back feels inauthentic to me. As the light comes in, the shadows recede. What I've come to realize is that when the shadows try to creep back in, they feel more uncomfortable than the light.

An exercise to help you stop hiding in plain sight is to look for evidence of joy in your life. Look for evidence of beauty all around you. To start the process, take a walk and notice each tree you pass. And when I say notice I mean really look at it and see all the different shades of green in the leaves. See the contour of the bark. Look closely at any flowers you see and take in their beauty. How does that feel inside? Notice the peacefulness and joy that start creeping in. By doing this you are accumulating more evidence of the beauty in life. The more you align with these feelings the less possible it is to hide in plain sight because you want to be out in the world experiencing it. Make sure on your walk to greet each person you see with a big smile and a kind word of "good morning," "good afternoon," or "have a nice day." When you do this, you are using your voice and being seen. You are also adding to the beauty of the world.

I invite you to embark upon your journey of stepping out of the shadows and to no longer hide in plain sight. Life is more joyful, peaceful, and beautiful there. I know you have the courage inside to do this. Just take a step and then another and see where you go. I'm here to say this is possible because I did it and I'm here with open ears and a loving heart to assist you and encourage you.

Visit my website at www.angelaunlimited.com to find out more about how we might connect.

Angela Design Keys to Living Out Loud

Key #10
Hiding in plain sight takes its toll on you. We are not meant to live like that. Instead, we are meant to live as who we truly are in our hearts. You know, the sparkly three-year-old version of us that lives inside regardless of our actual age. Dip into your soul and find the courage to start taking steps towards living a life of unlimited possibilities. You deserve and can have that life. I found my way to it and so can you!

For my personal message
Scan the QR Code with your smart phone
Or go to: https://youtu.be/0Gc45lY_qs8

Chapter Eleven

Living in the Shadows

Shadows seep into our lives when we are not living as either the best version of ourselves or as our authentic selves.
—Angela Wilson

Early in my career, when I was working on earning my accounting designation, I failed an exam. And I was fired on the spot. The managing partner at the company I worked for said he was sorry because he hated to lose me. I was a good staff person. But it was company policy.

How freaking discouraging is that when you are starting out? It all worked out for the best because I realized through that job and the next that I really didn't want to work for an accounting firm. I wanted to run a finance department in industry, so I obtained my designation when I was working as a controller for a manufacturing company. My doubt still held—actually, it increased—as the working environment was very toxic and I and others were routinely told how stupid we were. I believe the phrase used on a regular basis was "trained monkeys could do your jobs just as well as, if not better than you can."

This played out in my home life, too, because I felt I didn't measure up there, either. Oh, I tried every way I knew how but I always felt like I was inferior in every way. The shadow of doubt whispered in my ear all the time. It ramped up my inner chatter so high that I would leave myself in a weeping puddle on the floor because I didn't know how to cope. My home was supposed to be my sanctuary—or at least that was the vision I had in my mind at the time. What I didn't realize was that, as a young girl, I had built up many visions and expectations of what a home should be and how it should operate.

As an adult, when reality didn't match my visions and expectations, my shadow of doubt grew, as I felt it was my fault things hadn't worked out. I had to be doing something wrong and I had to fix it. I took the burden onto my shoulders. My darker shadow grew bigger, and I wound my now well-reinforced blankets of protection even tighter around me just to make it through each day. I couldn't see the light at that point. I existed in the shadows of my own life.

What is the first thought that jumps into your head when you hear the term "living in the shadows"? For me, Living in the Shadows means living anything less than the full authentic version of yourself. That's a fairly broad statement so let's break it down a bit. I've talked about a number of different elements already that go into living in the shadows, such as shame, losing your voice, listening to your inner chatter, hiding in plain sight, feeling "less than," and feeling like you don't matter. The protective layers we bury ourselves in are part of living in the shadows and they indicate that we are living in a state of surviving instead of *living*. We will talk more about surviving in a later chapter but for now, let's keep looking at shadows.

What do you notice when you see your shadow? It can be tall and thin or short and squat, depending on the angle of the sun. And if you are standing in the shadow of a building on a hot day, what do you notice? I sense it is cooler and dimmer there. Shadows are like a veil of darkness that aren't quite dark and not quite light. You can maneuver through them as their misty coolness swirls around you.

When something untoward is going to happen in a movie someone will typically come out of a shadow or some mist. This is where our fears, habits, and thoughts confine us. Is that a place you want to live in or operate from?

I spent many years in these shadows in the past. The fear, doubt, and shame I felt was almost debilitating at times, while at other times I could manage. Ah, there is an important distinction…I could manage. Managing is not living. I used to say I felt like I was trudging through life or slogging through mud. It wasn't pleasant and it is not the way life is supposed to be.

Doubting Everything

The shadow of doubt played a huge role in my life. I doubted myself about almost everything. Some would have said that I was self-conscious or that I had low self-esteem but those are by-products of doubt. The shadow of doubt keeps confidence on its outer edge, just out of reach. The shadow is elusive and cunning and as you try to step toward confidence your inner chatter pulls you back. Because I doubted myself so much, I gave my power away. I assumed everyone else was smarter than I was, and I would take what other people said as The Truth. I remember once relaying back to someone something they had told me that I thought was fact; they laughed at me and said, "I was only joking. I never thought you would think that was true." I responded, "but that's what you told me, and this is your area of expertise, and I trust you." From then on, my self-doubt increased because now I didn't think I knew fact from fiction, and I didn't want to get laughed at again. That story was repeated shortly afterwards in front of a group of friends, and everyone had a good laugh at my expense. I just shrugged and smiled and said, "what can I say?" I mean, after all, what *could* I say at that point?

The shadow of doubt for me was dark, long, and all-encompassing. It took a lot of time and courage to walk out of it, but I did it. That doesn't mean it just slipped away never to be seen again. You see, the problem is that these big shadows in our lives lurk in the background just waiting for us to be a bit "off," or let our inner chatter ramp up because we let our vibration/energy level drop. And then, if we aren't paying attention, they slither in, and we can feel the heaviness and the uncertainty inside us grow.

For me, the shadows are really part of the protective layers I spoke about earlier. You see, as I plastered on more protective layers the shadows cocooned in with me, lurking and watching for new cracks to invade so they could wrap themselves more tightly around me. But I wasn't paying attention to them because I didn't understand. I couldn't see them for what they were. Challenges kept mounting and when I couldn't fix them, I would ignore them and run away from them. Have you ever noticed you can't really run away from a shadow? It changes shape, but it keeps up with you, as it is firmly attached to you. I felt as though I spent every minute of every day trying to outrun my shadow. At work I would spend every minute proving that I was somehow worthy, proving that I was at least "adequate" for my job. I'm a university-educated woman and a designated accountant. I am ethical and conscientious and I'm a hard worker. Objectively speaking, I was more than "adequate" for my job. But that didn't matter because in my mind it was only a matter of time before someone realized I wasn't smart enough, and my job would be gone.

The shadows started to retreat when my former relationship ended, and I realized I was living so far off purpose I could no longer even see my path. I felt like a million miles away from it. I was in such a state I had to ask for help. Dealing with that life-altering event catalyzed me to make significant changes in my life. I began to gather the courage to listen to the whisper inside that had been telling me for years that "there is more to life, there is more to me." Each step I took and each new awareness I had led to new choices. I worked with a number of mentors and started to peel the shadows back from my true purpose in life and found my way back to my path. Sometimes in response to a compliment I would say, "but that's not special, that's just me." The answer my mentors always gave me was, "Correct but it is the 'just you' parts that make you special." It took a lot of courage for me to stay in those conversations and keep showing up and ask questions. I knew I couldn't go on living the way I had been living and I had to change in order to survive. I also came to realize that I didn't want to just survive anymore. I wanted to live my life fully and be who I was meant to be. And through it all I came to realize that asking for assistance is not a sign of weakness, or a sign that you are "less than" others. Asking for assistance shows that you want something more. I came to realize we are not meant to go through life as a solo act. There is an old saying that affirms that it takes a village to raise a child. I think that phrase needs to be changed because even as adults we need a village around us in order to thrive. A lone wolf in the wild can survive but it is a tough and lonely road. A wolf in a pack thrives.

One of the biggest lessons I've learned on my journey so far is that we need community in order to fully step out of the shadows and live our life on purpose. It has to be the "right" community, though, one whose members can see you for who you are and embrace your uniqueness. People in that type of community can assist us when we stumble a bit—and we all stumble. I've also learned that when the shadows sneak back in and I isolate myself from the people who see me the most, it feels awful, and I can't stay in that space for very long anymore. I've learned that my place is not hiding in the shadows but standing in the light and being Angela.

We are each on a journey. Life is not a "fix it and we're done" project, nor is it a "fixer-upper." If you open yourself to the possibility that you are here for a purpose and your journey serves that purpose, then each day is an adventure and not a task to get somewhere. When you live your life that way, standing fully in your light, the shadows fall behind you.

I've had something bothering me for a while and I finally figured out what it was about. Maybe this will resonate with you, too. I kept trying to stick to a regular exercise routine, but I just couldn't do it. I would say, "Okay this week I'm going to…" And it didn't happen. I became angry with myself and beat myself up for not following through. What I realized this morning as I was journalling and letting my thoughts flow onto the page was that for me exercise is wrapped up in the shadow of doubt. See if you can meet me there:

I started by writing "I'm curious why this seems to be an issue for me and yet it comes so naturally to others. Did I miss the natural exercise chromosome?" I wrote a bit more and let it noodle around for a while and then I began to write about taking the pressure off myself and changing my inner talk from, "*I have to exercise every day,*" to "*Why not start exercising twice a week and build from there?*" I felt somewhat better as I had eased my mind and I was letting my heart lead: my heart knows that when I put too much pressure on myself things go sideways. So, I shifted gears and started writing about Happy Inner Magnificence Day which is what I call Wednesday. I didn't like it when people called Wednesday "Hump Day." I understood the reasoning, but I thought we could do better than that, so I changed it. I use the phrasing when I post on Facebook and there is a blog on my website www.angelaunlimited.com that explains why I came up with it. Shifting the topic of my writing allowed me to write from my inner knowing instead of from my head. I wrote "Why are some choices harder to commit to? Probably because they are more deeply rooted in our old programming. Damn, could that be the whole exercise thing? Does this come out of that old "I'm not good at that" place? There is something about this that is ringing true. Holy shit, that one was really buried in there! Okay, time to shed some more light on that one and see where it takes me." You can see how I use writing to process thoughts that are uncomfortable or whirling around in my head too much. It's even an orderly process. I start writing about the item and then I let it expand.

If I get stuck, then I shift my writing to something else that is more peaceful and then typically the underlying thought/pattern/habit pops out. I don't always solve my issue in one go because if it is something that has been buried deep it isn't going to run away in a few minutes. But now I'm aware of the underlying "I'm not good at" shadow and can address it by meeting it in the light of choice, courage, and change.

Journalling might not be your favourite tool to understanding but I find it very helpful so maybe give it a try. If it doesn't work, look for another avenue. Maybe it's drawing for you, so let your artistic side meander while thoughts are flowing through you. The idea is to open your mind so you can hear your inner knowing. That's what I do with journalling. I let the words tumble onto the page so they can sort themselves out. You might also have a conversation with someone you trust, someone who will let you talk and through the talking figure things out. You don't want to do this with someone who is going to judge you, make you wrong, or try to fix you. You want them to assist you to find your unique way of processing these things.

You may be thinking, "*that's all well and good Angela but I'm comfortable where I am. I know how to navigate this way.*" And my response is, "I totally get that and understand it. But I would also guess you've heard a whisper inside that there is more to you, more to life. I doubt you would be reading this book if you hadn't. In some of my darkest days I would think to myself "*I thought life was supposed to be easier and happier than this.*" Well, it *is* supposed to be easier and happier than it seems when you are pushing a huge boulder uphill: sooner or later you slip or get tired, and that boulder rolls back on you. So, when that happened to me, I mustered up my courage to go on the journey of remembering who I was because, to be honest, not being me was tearing me apart.

I recommend you give the exercise of journalling a try. Start with the question you are asking yourself or the thing that is upsetting you, making you angry, or making you doubt yourself. Write it on the page. If you find writing sentences stressful you can also write this question in the middle of a piece of paper and then start writing words in random places all over the page. Be creative with it and don't engage with your thoughts too much. Let them tumble onto the page and look for patterns in them. It will assist you to see the deep layers of the issue without taking you way down a rabbit hole.

Angela's Design Keys for Living Out Loud

Key #11
Stepping out of the shadows allows us to live as the best version of ourselves. It lets us step into our lives with confidence and clarity. When you are standing in the light instead of the shadows you thrive in life, and it becomes full and joyful.

For my personal message
Scan the QR Code with your smart phone
Or go to: https://youtu.be/MuXqDEYaSXc

Chapter Twelve

Wanting to Fit In

*Trying to fit in represents another shadow we hide
in to try and prove our self-worth. Trust me, you
are already worthy. Feel into the truth of that!*
—Angela Wilson

As a kid I would have given anything to be one of the pretty, petite girls who were great at gymnastics, sports, or what felt like everything. I could compete in a number of activities adequately well in those days, but I never quite found my groove when it came to organized sports. My happy place was the skating arena where almost every Friday and Saturday night I could go and lose myself on the rink. While I skated, I'd listen to the music and feel free, like I wasn't being judged. I'd go ice skating in the winter and roller skating in the summer. Even now the memory brings a smile to my face. I still wanted to try to fit in at the arena: I was not one of the girls the boys would chase and that bothered me sometimes. But I could let it all slip away, even if only for a few minutes as I glided across the ice and powered through the corners.

In high school, I felt like I fit in a little more because by that time I had become more adept at shifting to match those around me. I was still not one of the popular girls and I was never asked out on dates. I had my main group of friends and I'm proud and grateful to say that a few of them are still in my life today. At the time, though, I even felt like a bit of an outsider with my good friends because I was bused to school and that made hanging out after school and participating in activities like everyone else more challenging, if not impossible. I had to make sure I caught the bus.

On weekends I didn't see my friends because I lived in a small town 15-20 minutes away from the town my school was in, and my parents didn't feel it was necessary to drive me in to hang out with my friends. What's more, in those days if I wanted to call a friend who lived near the school my parents would have had to pay long-distance fees, so yakking with my friends was not an option either. And yes, I am old enough that there were no cell phones and no internet in those days, so I couldn't email, text or message my friends.

Have you ever wanted more than anything to fit in? I have spent my whole life trying to do exactly that and still at times today I slide back into that misguided spot. We learn at a young age we should have friends to play with and that we should be part of a group. If you don't have a lot of friends, then you aren't popular, and people make fun of you and tease you. I experienced a lot of this when I was a young girl. In elementary school I was taller than everyone else and not just by a little bit; being branded with that odious nickname of "Big Bertha" really did a number on me. My mother made me wear dresses most of the time—while the other girls were allowed to wear jeans—and I had short hair at a time when long hair was considered significantly more fashionable.

Unwelcome in the popular groups at school I shifted between the other groups like a chameleon. I blended in the best I could until inevitably I had to adjust my behaviour again to remain in the group. Sometimes I couldn't remain in a group because fitting in was simply too hard. I was desperate to be liked.

It was all a powder keg waiting to blow me into Tease-ville. I'm sure the kids who called me Big Bertha just figured they were having fun. The problem was, it was at my expense, and the awful feelings that went along with the nickname stayed in my subconscious mind until I was in my 50s.

So why are we talking about fitting in and the things that happened while I was in elementary school and high school? Well, it is because during those years a lot of beliefs formed for me and maybe for you, too. I had a very clear picture in my mind that I did not fit in, and I recognized that somehow, I didn't "measure up" to the other girls around me. It's a tough time for a young girl and I suspect you may have had similar feelings or at least can identify with them in some way. The problem was that I spent so much time desperately wanting and trying to fit in that I was never Angela. I was the Angela I needed to be in order to fit into the group I was trying on in the moment.

When we shapeshift ourselves as we bounce between our own "home base" and the groups we embrace it becomes very confusing, and we start forgetting who we are. It also takes a large energetic toll on us as it is hard to keep all the versions of who we're trying to be straight. I became very adept at the type of "personality gymnastics" required to flip between versions of myself and over time I probably became an Olympic medallist in the practice. But the price to me, which you might be feeling as well, was very steep.

Trying to Fit In

The price increased the older I became as it took more effort to try and fit in. You would think that once I became an adult none of this would matter anymore but it did. Fitting in became a way of life. I lost who I truly, authentically, was and then I felt like I didn't fit anywhere. In my mid-twenties as I mentioned I was in a relationship in which over time I lost myself. I thought this was a role I could jump in and play but I had so many expectations of what a good partner was supposed to look like that I couldn't relax into "me." Over time my inner chatter screamed at me about how inadequate I was and gave me evidence I didn't fit in my own home. My partner and I would go out for dinner with friends, and I would always be the odd man out because most of our friends were in the same profession as my partner. I sat while the conversations passed me by. I would jump in when I could, but I didn't understand the topics being discussed.

I will be honest: I can still struggle with this sometimes today and if I don't watch myself that fearful shadow of wanting to fit in can start slinking in. It's an ongoing effort to believe in me. The members of one of the groups I'm involved with refer to themselves as being part of "the Not Belonging Club."

Well, the icky part of my brain that wants to be heard can sometimes say, "look, you don't even fit with the Not Belonging Club." The other old pattern that calls out to me at times is, "aren't I old enough yet to just not give a damn?" These are the holdover mind games from my past. They are not the truth but there was a time they felt like it.

Most of the time now I don't care anymore if I fit in or not. I am me and I have to be who I am at my heart level because I have learned that fitting in is not my journey.

But how did I go from feeling invisible, having lost my sense of self, and having completely messed myself up with mind games, to who I am today? It was a journey that took some time, and I was able to do it with a lot of love, support, and tapping into my courageous heart. No one can do this for you. Sorry, but it is a choice you have to make. As I reclaimed who I was and remembered who I was in my heart I realized *that* Angela had not been seen in a really long time and it was scary. I had no idea where I was headed but I knew in my heart it was the way to go. I look back now, and I don't even recognize myself. Which makes sense because I wasn't me. And the reality was that it was impossible for me to stay in that spot because there was more to my journey. Just like there is more to your journey.

I've mentioned before I always felt like there was more to me even in my darkest hours and I suspect you have that same feeling rumbling deep within. And that is why you picked up this book. My journey was always meant to bring me to a place where I could be of assistance to others. That is why I had the experiences I had, so I can now say them out loud and assist others going through similar experiences. My wish in writing this book, in my speaking engagements, and in the courses I offer, is to be a catalyst for someone else to make the choice to embrace who they are and not have to live for decades the way I did.

Some people may think not fitting in is *no big deal* and people who feel that way should just get over it. I know from experience it isn't that simple and that the pain goes way deeper and impacts us in ways we didn't even know about until we start embracing the real "us" again. It isn't an overnight fix, but it is completely doable. The first thing we have to realize is there is nothing wrong with us and there never was. What happened was that our ears and brain filtered and processed the world around us in a perceptively unproductive way and our inner chatter played games that made us feel invisible; we believed it was impossible to change. This is where the first real bout of courage comes in.

You must make the choice that you want something different. Even if you don't know what that is yet. Make the choice for change. That choice alone opens a number of doors to other possibilities. The next step is to not do this alone. You have to make the choice to let people in. That might seem like an impossible feat but as you start leaving space for someone to enter it will be okay. Trust your instincts, as to who those people should be. I know it will be scary at first because the other thing you probably stopped doing some time ago was listening to your instincts. I know that happened to me. Now I know better. My instincts don't lead me astray. It is my inner chatter that sends me down the path to Bizarre Land.

It might seem strange to talk about courage and listening to your instincts. Some people think it is just natural to hear/feel your instincts, but it isn't. That is why I said it would take courage. The first piece of courage will be to speak up and actually use your voice out loud. The next bit of courage will be a building block as you test/try listening to your instincts. Your instincts can also be called your inner knowing. It is the voice deep inside you. For me, it comes through as a whispered knowing from my heart. Others sense/hear a voice which is full of guidance and wisdom.

When we have stopped listening to and trusting our instincts it takes a bit of time for us to remember what this voice sounds or feels like. At first, it is easy to miss because we have trained ourselves to ignore it and we listen to our bratty inner chatter yelling at us instead.

As an exercise to start listening to your inner knowing/instincts and to start using your courage to speak out loud I invite you to do the following: take some time every day to quiet your mind. It doesn't have to be a long time. Start with one minute and work from there. When we are quieting our mind, we are stopping our inner chatter from running the show. To do this, just concentrate on your breath.

Let any thoughts you have just wash through. Don't engage with them because, initially, they will represent your ego trying to get your attention. After doing this a few times start paying attention to the other thoughts—or the voice—that come through to you. As I said, mine is like a whisper. Yours may be a feeling inside. Don't judge it, just sit with it. Let those thoughts linger if they would like to. You will know the difference when you are in stillness. As you gain momentum with this exercise start voicing what you are hearing out loud. It might look like this: out loud, in the presence of other people, you can say, "I'm feeling like I would like to move my life in a different direction. I'm not sure yet what that looks like, but I would love to travel more and explore other places."

The actual thoughts will be unique to you. Be prepared because if you haven't used your voice in some time people might challenge you on what you say. It's all okay. Just smile and say, "there are lots of thoughts percolating and I'm sifting through them. I do like the idea of traveling more, though, going forward." Use your courage to stay in charge of your voice. Remember, people are going to judge, and you don't need to buy into their judgements.

Life is a journey. Fitting in is really just a construct that society has made for us, and it's based in fear. What I have learned is that when I am completely me and allow myself to have fun, be creative, and live life full-on, there are lots of people around because like-minded people come into my circle. The biggest realization is that the only place it is important to fit in is in your heart. When you fit in to your heart and live in your authenticity and integrity, Life is blissful. Other people in your life are playmates and that is it.

The dictionary defines fitting in as being "socially compatible with other members of a group." That is not the societal definition. The societal one goes a little more like…you feel that you belong to a particular group, and you are accepted by that group. Being part of a community that embraces who you are is fantastic.

But at what price do you want to be accepted? The moment you must veer off from your inner knowing to be part of that community or group it is time to make a change. You deserve to live your life as the full authentic you. It takes courage. I'm committed to not wavering on this as I feel strongly that the only way for me to live lies in being true to me and I love having playmates. So come join me and let yourself shine!

Angela's Design Keys for Living Out Loud

Key #12
It is not your journey to fit in. Your journey is to be 1000% you all the time. It takes courage and choices to live in this space. It is worth it! You are worth it!

For my personal message
Scan the QR Code with your smart phone
Or go to: https://youtu.be/uJkEAj_8tb4

Chapter Thirteen

Surviving Life is not Living

> *To be the best version of you, you cannot simply survive your life; you have to LIVE your life.*
> —Angela Wilson

Until the last few years, I always had a "to do list" a mile long and it seemed like for every one item I accomplished I would add four more. When we do that, we are trying to survive our "to do list." I also put the needs of my clients ahead of my own for years and I worked crazy hours. I had friends who knew not to contact me at certain times of the year because I was too busy to be able to do anything fun.

So, I was surviving my work schedule and surviving my clients' needs. I made sure that dinner was cooked, lunches were packed, and the house was relatively tidy in case someone stopped by. So, I was surviving my home. I would take classes on topics that interested me, but I was always exhausted; the homework was always a struggle and the classes left me feeling "less than" because I couldn't keep up. I would show up and do assignments, but I never felt like I was all in because I was surviving the class. When you add up each of the pieces, I was surviving my life.

What does that do to someone who is a visionary type of person and comes from a place of abundance at heart? It depletes them because they are on a hamster wheel, always trying to "get there," always trying to get things done, always trying to take care of things, but feeling inside like they are failing miserably. In those days, I wasn't taking care of myself. I had zero creativity because every time I tried to do something creative it just felt like something else to weigh me down.

I remember often feeling there had to be something creative inside me. I remember saying the words "I must have *some* kind of creative bone in my body." It haunted me. You see, people joked that I had no artistic talent. And I had never been praised in art class. I also couldn't write powerfully as a child. And people weren't shy about telling me about it. That messaging lived inside me, and it played itself out because, ultimately, I was surviving my life so hard, I couldn't get to the glimmer of my creativity. In fact, I had hidden it deep within. Why would I bring creativity out into the sunlight and try new things when I'd been mocked about my creative abilities my whole life? I remember being shocked when I got my first assignment back during a creative writing class, I took in my late 30s. I thought, "look at that, I didn't suck!"

As you can see, while I was so busy surviving my life, I blocked a lot of emotion. I used to scoff at people mentioning they needed time for self-care. "Are you kidding?" I would think. "Buck up, and get the job done." Of course, my thinking about that all changed as I moved forward on my journey. You see, I thought self-care was an indulgence and "real" people didn't need it. I had to get to a clear understanding of what it meant for me and hear it in words that made sense to me. The final penny dropped on this notion recently as I finally made the connection. I would get my hair and nails done but I never saw that as self-care.

These were important to me, and they were scheduled into my calendar just like a client appointment would be. They were another task. What I understand now is that they are essential to me living a thriving life. I had been in survival mode a long time and had not been taking care of myself in any real way. It took some time to shed this mindset block. But here's an interesting point: the more you shift your thinking and actions from surviving to thriving the more you will want to take care of yourself because you see your value.

And we tend to take care of things and people we value. Are you ready for a breakthrough on this? It will take some courage, but I know you have it…you can do this!

When someone asks you how you are, have you ever said, "I'm surviving"? When we say this aloud, we give off an energy akin to scraping the bottom of a barrel and it puts us in a state of energetic depletion. If we are surviving, we cannot thrive because those concepts are at opposite ends of the spectrum of living the life you deserve. Your best life. My hope in writing this book is to support us all in swinging from any aspect of surviving to thriving and the sooner we do it the better. It takes choice and courage, and it takes shifting your belief and tapping into the courage in your heart.

When I talk about surviving, I'm not just talking about trudging through one day after another, putting one foot in front of the other and hoping to make it to the next dull day. My guess is that if that is how you are managing your life you no longer want that, and you are looking for another way to do things. There is another type of surviving that is just as limiting. It's the type of surviving where we rush madly around all day making sure we accomplish everything on our "to do list" and taking care of everyone around us…but at the end of it we have nothing left over for ourselves. We put everyone else first and nine times out of ten we don't take care of ourselves and there we are, running on fumes. In my world, I call that "surviving better."

When we are surviving our lives we are coming from a place of scarcity. Even though my outlook on life stemmed from an arena of scarcity for a good part of my life, my heart was still abundant. It created a conflict within me. The shadow of scarcity was powerful. I started giving up on some of my dreams, one of which had been to visit Serengeti National Park in Africa. I longed for it, but I also *knew* it was not going to happen. As you know now, I eventually grew out of that place of scarcity and welcomed that trip into my life (see Chapter Seven to read that part again!). To this day I can close my eyes and be back there in a heartbeat. When I look at pictures, I can remember vivid details. I wouldn't have any of those memories if I had stayed in survival mode.

One of the biggest things that surviving my life took away from me was the joy of dreaming. I even got to a place where I didn't know how to dream. I was so deep in survival mode that I just wanted to get through the day. The end of the relationship I mentioned triggered a huge change in my life.

After some time and many tears, I realized the relationship couldn't have continued. I had lost too many parts of me. You see, I could only survive because my internal dialogue, formed from the messages I had heard about myself growing up, and continued to hear in other relationships, reflected a person far removed from who I truly am. I had to shift my thinking and it made me examine everything there was to examine. This didn't happen overnight, but it also didn't take decades, either. Maybe you might see the value of making choices to shift out of survival mode before you have a catastrophic reason that forces you to do so.

When I got back in touch with who I was things started to change, and they changed rapidly. I went on my dream trip to Tanzania, and the love of my life entered my world. I remember one day early on Gord asked what my dreams were for my life. I was stumped because my mind—my egoic inner-chatter-mind—told me I didn't dream; it was still trying to hold onto "surviving," just in case. But as time progressed, I started to dream more, and the dreams started to form into reality. When you start allowing that process to happen you shift from surviving to thriving and you shed any scarcity mentality lurking in the background.

We Are on a Journey

Again, this is a process, and we are on a journey. On occasion, if you aren't paying attention, the old survival mode might try to kick in and you might let yourself wander off your path. When this happens, to me, I look back on the evidence that shows me how far I have come and how much my life has changed. I generally start by thinking of one thing I'm grateful for in my life. My husband is at the top of that list because meeting him and being in a relationship with him was a dream that definitely came true.

A daily gratitude practice is key. Being grateful for our lives, our blessings, those near and dear to us, and ourselves, is incredibly powerful. There is no right or wrong way to do this. I found it hard in the beginning: someone suggested I write down 10 things every day that I was grateful for, and they all had to be different. The first few were easy but then it was challenging. Trust me, in the beginning I tried to get it "right" but when I made it my own it was more meaningful and more impactful.

I now follow a gratitude practice every day. It varies depending on the day and what I have going on. Sometimes at night before I hand over my day and go to sleep, I allow as many "I am grateful for" thoughts to flow through my mind. It brings a peaceful end to my day. Other times if my morning has a busy early start, I will take a few minutes before I climb out of bed and allow "I am grateful for" statements to flow through. I tried for a while to keep a gratitude journal, which works amazingly well for some people, but I found it stressful as it was one more thing, I felt I had to get right. The right book, the right pen, the right thoughts, and the right time—because it didn't work for me to do this as I was drawing my day to a close. I found the best practice for me was to incorporate gratitude when I'm journalling. At the end of each journalled session, I conclude with a few lines—okay, often several—about things I'm grateful for. I find it grounding and it brings me back into my heart as it reminds me how blessed I am, how far I have come, and how wonderful life can be. On the rare days I don't journal as I mentioned I let my grateful thoughts float through in the morning and/or before bed.

I suggest giving a gratitude practice a try. You can do it the way I have described or keep a separate journal just for that purpose. Whatever works for you. Try implementing the following into your daily routine. First, choose whether you are going to try morning or night to begin. Next, choose if you are going to start by writing or going through the thoughts in your mind. I always find it more impactful when you can add in more senses so give writing a try. Third, write as many "I am grateful for…" statements as you can.

The reason I also recommend writing them is because when doubt creeps in you can go back and look at the statements you have written. It is added evidence of how far you have come. And, finally, be consistent with this practice every day. It will become more fluid and the energy you are building will grow exponentially.

One thing I have learned is that when you are in a state of gratitude every day it is difficult to be in a place of scarcity and survival. Being consciously in a state of gratitude shifts our outlook on life and it allows us to move past surviving to thriving. I hope you will consider this and give it a try. It may feel challenging initially. But as you continue with it you will see how much you truly have to be grateful for, including the magnificent life you have and are building.

Angela's Design Keys to Living Out Loud

Key #13
Practicing gratitude everyday grounds us in our hearts and allows us to be free of the shadow of scarcity. It also shifts us from surviving to thriving in our lives. Thriving is where the magic happens, and gratitude is a key element to that magic.

For my personal message
Scan the QR Code with your smart phone
Or go to: https://youtu.be/p9MgmIjX0-A

Chapter Fourteen

Intentional Dreaming

> *We can dream a million dreams, however, if we are not dreaming about them intentionally they are nothing more than wings and prayers. There is nothing wrong with those types of dreams. However, the ones that pull us forward and change our lives have intention and action behind them.*
> —Angela Wilson

I've mentioned I met the love of my life. I have also said he did not come in on a horse as a knight to save me. I didn't need to be saved and it was not his job. We found each other at the prefect time in our lives. I had come a long way in my journey when Gord came into my life. I still had a way to go and honestly, every day is still a step in my journey. I'm just further down the path now and my lessons have changed for where I am now. Life is not "one and done," my friend. It is a continuous journey of discovery, curiosity, and joy. Gord came into my life to love me. All of me. We tell everyone that we are partners in everything and that is 100% true.

So, you may be wondering why I mentioned intentional dreaming and then started to discuss Gord. You see, when I was trying to figure myself out, initially I wondered, *"Who is ever going to love me? I'm broken and damaged."* As I continued to heal and talk out loud and journal like a fiend, I gained the knowledge that this was not true. I was lovable; I just hadn't met the right person for me. In my journalling I often wrote about the man who would come into my life. I wrote about his family, our feelings for each other, and how we would treat each other. As I did this the picture became clearer and clearer until one day, I met Gord.

I had gone out with a few men and none of them represented what I was looking for. I know it sounds cliché, but I had decided I was good being on my own and if someday the man I was looking for walked into my life great, but I was done searching. I knew in my heart he would walk in if and when the time was right. Not long after that I was invited to a party.

Actually, it was a birthday party for Gord and one of his friends. I was there because a colleague had asked me to go with her as her husband was unable to attend. At first I said, "No, I'm not going to a birthday party for some guy I don't even know." She insisted and I said, "Fine as long as you check to make sure it's okay with him." She did, and I went with her to the party. Here is a funny aside. I was not supposed to be in town that weekend, however, circumstances changed and, synchronistically, I was. And the party turned out to be just a couple of blocks from my house. Talk about a cosmic redirect! I was introduced to Gord and a number of other people. A while later I was listening to the conversation going on and I heard someone ask Gord if today was his birthday. He said, "No my birthday is on Wednesday." I couldn't believe my ears when I heard him say that. I spoke up and said, "I hate to interrupt but did you just say your birthday is on Wednesday?" He answered, "Yes." I said, "Well that's *my* birthday. So, I guess this party is for me, too."

We laughed and talked further. It was so easy to talk to him. I left the party thinking what a nice time and what a great guy. I'm glad I went. He left the party thinking, "I want to get to know her." I hadn't realized that until after when we started spending time together. About a week later he orchestrated a meeting between a group of his friends, the person who had introduced us, and me. I remember wondering at the time why my schedule was such an important piece of information in the planning of this event. That's when a dear friend said, "Hello! He likes you." My answer was "Oh." I honestly didn't know what to say. What I did do was go out with everyone, and Gord and I talked for hours. It was in the conversation, and the ease of being able to talk to Gord, that I realized I had found my soul mate.

I had intentionally "dreamt" about Gord, and he came into my life. I didn't know it would be him specifically. He does have all the qualities I dreamt about and that's what is key. Dreams are such an important part of our lives. They pull us forward and give us something to work toward. They can be big or small and be short-term or long-term. The key is to dream.

I'll give you an exercise to work on your dreams: write down at least one dream you have. After you write it down, I want you to go back to what you wrote and I want you to fill in as vividly as possible any sights, colours, smells, sounds, and/or tastes as you can. Be explicit. I want you to draw a fulsome picture of this dream. Then I want you to start visualizing this dream with all the detail you wrote down. If more comes to mind, add it in. Make sure when you are done to add any additional ideas into your written work. When we do that, the dreams become more tactile, more real. I do this exercise with my clients as I believe it is important to our journey toward standing strong in our life.

When we dream like this and make it this real, we are moving toward our dreams. We can then start taking action to move toward them. The initial action is to take any small step you can toward your dream and be open to possibilities as they show up. When I say "take small steps" that could be something like the example I just shared about going out and being social. And "being open to possibilities" means being open to meeting new people and seeing how things transpire. Also, don't be attached to an exact outcome. Hold it loosely. Here's an example of what I mean: I had always gone out with men who were taller than me so my automatic assumption was that my ultimate partner would also be taller than me. Gord and I are close to the same height. Now, if I were super attached to the idea that he had to be taller than me I would have overlooked an amazing man and missed out on the chance for a superb relationship.

When we get clear on what our dreams are, and we start moving toward them, this will assist us in the decisions and choices we make in our lives. You see, our dreams give us another piece of the roadmap for our journey. The fun part about our dreams is that they fill in parts of the roadmap, but they still leave us lots of room to play along the way. Hence, it's important to be open to possibilities and see where we go. Life is an adventure and the more curious we are and the more we dream, the fuller and more adventurous it becomes.

When was the last time you dreamt? I don't mean at night when you are sleeping. I mean consciously thinking about where you want to go and what you want in your life. We stop dreaming for many reasons. Sometimes we don't think we deserve our dreams, or we don't realize that option is available to us given where we currently are in our life, or we have simply forgotten how to dream—after all, we are no longer children. Just because we are adults doesn't mean we no longer get to dream. It is even more important to dream as an adult so that you can keep that wonder and splendour burning inside. As with everything else, our dreams will change over time because we change and therefore our dreams need to evolve and uplevel with us. Dreaming and then creating a plan to get there is rewarding! I hope you will embrace the exercise and continue with it. I have had some pretty amazing experiences that started as the small seed of a dream.

Angela's Design Keys to Living Out Loud

Key #14
Dreams are a magnificent part of life. Embrace them. Go after them. Live fully in the magic and you will be amazed at who and what comes into your life. It starts with you opening to possibility, taking some action, and getting really clear on what you want. You get to choose!

For my personal message
Scan the QR Code with your smart phone
Or go to: https://youtu.be/JOnIuqKbRcA

Chapter Fifteen

Choices. We Have Them!

*When you are living in the shadows of fear,
doubt, and shame you feel like you have no
choices. You do. Your choices are just hiding,
waiting for you to see them.*
—Angela Wilson

I jumped at the first job offer I received coming out of school because it was a big deal to me that one of the Big Five accounting firms wanted me. I didn't think through what might be best for me or what *I* actually wanted. I jumped at it because my perception was that other people would see where I worked and somehow that would elevate my worth. It didn't, but I thought that was the only choice possible for me. I didn't realize I could have made any choice I wanted to make. The same thing happened with my first home. I chose it based on my perception of what I was supposed to do or thought I was expected to do. I didn't ever stop, stand strong, and say, "I don't have to follow that line of thinking. I can make my own choice."

As the years went by, and my experiences mounted, I rarely felt like I had a choice. I worked to pay the bills, have a house, and have some fun. The first time I felt like I had a real choice in my career was when I decided to open my accounting practice and work with several different organizations as head of their finance departments. I felt like I was choosing my life because I was doing something outside of the norm. It was one of the best choices I ever made because it set me on a completely different path than I had originally envisioned for my career., After a while, however, I didn't feel like I had a lot of choices; my business became a job and I felt like my days were run by several people and my time didn't seem my own. I forgot I could choose to say, "no."

When my previous relationship ended, I didn't think I had any choices. The world seemed so bleak. I realized quickly, however, that I had a ton of choices. I had heard that "we choose our lives" before, but I had never felt I could do it, perhaps because I had become lost in myself. I was buried so deep within that it seemed there were no choices to be made—I just allowed things to happen to me. The biggest choice I had to make was around how I was going to move forward. What did I want my life to look like in the wake of this horrendous experience? I was revamping my life completely and I learned very quickly that all the choices were mine to make. It was a complete eye-opener for me!

I took steps to remember who I was inside and to get back in touch with the journey I was on in life. I learned a lot about myself and realized all the choices I get to make daily. One of the most important choices I realized I had was around how I'm going to show up in the world. What an eye-opener that was for me! Honestly, it had never crossed my mind before. I was so entrenched in my day-to-day life it had never occurred to me that I could choose to show up a different way. The other thing that I realized during this time was that I could choose how I was going to react to things. As time went on, I realized I had choices available to me in all areas of my life.

It was a fascinating time in my life for sure. I'm hoping what I'm sharing will resonate and assist you to make choices in your life so you can avoid some of the pitfalls I landed in. As I've mentioned, I have no regrets because all my experiences have brought me to where I am today, and I am loving life these days.

Have you felt throughout most of your life that you've had choices? When your mind was yelling all those seemingly hateful negative things at you did you feel like you had a choice to turn the volume down or shut it off? Did you feel like you had a choice to show your emotions...or not? I'm betting you answered, "No, I didn't feel like I had a choice," to at least some of those questions. I'm betting you at times felt like life was happening *to* you. In reality, when we are in these perceptively negative mindsets, and having experiences we don't enjoy, it is hard to see we can choose to change them.

I remember when my inner chatter was at its worst: I had no idea how to stop it on my own. Honestly, I thought I was losing my mind. I figured there was something wrong with me because I didn't see anyone else going through the same thing. The other side of the coin is, of course, I didn't see anyone else going through the same thing because I never said anything aloud about what I was experiencing so no one knew what I was dealing with, either. Maybe they were experiencing the same thing as me! We live in our own protected hell and are afraid to let others see what a mess we are.

Did you grow up thinking that there was an unspoken order to things? I did. You went to school. You were supposed to get good grades. You would go on to university or college. You would graduate with good grades. You would get a job. You would get married. You would have children. You would buy a house. You would work until you were 65 and then retire. Does any of that sound familiar? Does it feel like there are a lot of choices within that structure? Well, there are some choices available, but there are limitations, as well. When you are in elementary or high school you can't pick the school you attend or the friends you have as these are typically vetted by your parents to make sure they are suitable. Okay, so maybe your choices start when you get your first job in high school? Well, maybe not, because the job needs to be suitable, and you need to be able to get there. Hmmm…so suitability and location limit your choices. Can you see how easy it is for us to think we don't have choices?

Okay, let's progress this one on a bit. You could choose your university or college from among the ones that accepted your application. Did you make that choice on your own? Did you go to the school that made your heart sing or did you attend the one that was most appropriate, or that your parents wanted you to attend? At this stage, though, you could choose your friends. After all, now you were an adult. Did you choose wisely, or did you choose to befriend at least a couple of people because you knew it would annoy your parents? So, at this stage in life, maybe we felt like we had some choices, but it was still a bit of a game, wasn't it?

Oh, just before we move forward to the next phase I have to ask: during your school years did you rebel against the system? Did you rebel against your parents? To me this rebellion—which some view as a rite of passage on the way to adulthood—is more of an expression of feeling like we have no choices. So, we do things to try and exert ourselves. Sometimes it pans out and sometimes it doesn't. I didn't take high school all that seriously. After all, the messaging I had heard was that I didn't measure up and I wasn't very good at anything—so, seriously, why would I try? That was part of my rebellion. I received decent grades, and I was able to get into university. But university was a little more challenging because I didn't have good study habits. At the end of the day, I made it through, and I received my Honours Bachelor's degree.

That being said, absolutely every step of our lives involves choices. We choose our responses to the choices our parents make for us, and we choose to either stay stuck in a situation or move forward from it. If I had realized I had choices as a kid, a teenager, or an adult in my early 20s I wonder what those experiences would have been like? But would I want to change them? Would you? I know I wouldn't. The experiences I have had made me the person I am today and I'm truly grateful for them.

Job, Marriage, Children, and House

So, let's briefly jump to the next few items on life's itinerary. Job, marriage, children, and house. Now, here is where some people think they are starting to make choices, and, in fact, they have nothing but choices at this stage, and others feel that most of their world is beyond their control and there are no choices. Here is what I know from my own experience: it was at this point in my life starting out as an adult—getting my first real job, my first real relationship, and buying my first home—where I felt I had many choices and where I felt I had no choices. I was in such a quandary at the time.

So, what does life look like when you realize you have choices? Well, for me it became more joyful and purposeful. I realized I could choose how to show up in the world. I could choose what I was going to do with my time. Who I was going to spend time with. How I was going to view people and situations. How I was going to treat myself. The last one was another big one for me. Throughout the years I had not been very kind to myself. Even now, at times, I catch myself putting others first and talking negatively to myself. The difference, though, is that I now know I have a choice so when that starts to happen, I put a stop to it quickly and make a different choice.

If someone had told me a few years ago that I could have chosen to change my career, I would have thought they were crazy. I figured I would continue with my accounting practice until it was time to retire. Interestingly enough, retirement to me now seems like such a funny, arbitrary notion, as well. There is no set time to retire. You get to choose! You can do it when the time is right for you!

When I look at things through the lens of today, I realize I did make choices in the past, but they were unconscious choices. Now my choices are conscious and deliberate. My choices feed who I am and how I want to show up in the world. Taking a stand for who we are and living within our integrity, authenticity, and values is what showing up in the world is all about. When we show up in the world, we make the choice to not meander through life. This goes hand in hand with showing the world who we are because we are choosing to be seen. When I did this, it also released my voice, which I now choose to use fully in my life. Showing up in the world, being seen, and using our voices can be scary but it is completely worth the effort.

Here's an exercise for you: for one week each day, be aware of the choices around you. Look for them and don't hide from them. Examine your thoughts surrounding these choices. Are the thoughts helpful or judgemental? If they are judgemental stop and revise your thoughts, making them helpful for your choice at hand. If it is easier write, the thoughts down and rework the words.

Because if you allow judgemental thoughts to continue when you are looking at the choices you have, they undermine your ability to make a choice. They will squash your courage and we want to use our courage to dive into seeing and making choices. By doing this exercise you are breaking the habit of hiding from your choices and thinking you don't have any. Give it a try. See by the end of the week how you are noticing more choices available to you and that they are becoming easier to make.

Navigating our choices can sometimes feel daunting. I think that is why sometimes we feel we don't have any choices; it is easier to survive in the status quo and not stick our heads above the surface of life. But is that the way life is supposed to be? I know my answer to that is, "No!" Life is supposed to be much more meaningful, joyful, peaceful, and beautiful. I suspect you might feel the same way, or you wouldn't have picked up this book. I also suspect you are looking for more out of life and you know there is more to you than what you have been experiencing.

Guess what? There *is* more to you. And I know without a doubt you have the courage to make the choices you need to make in order to change your life. It all starts by choosing something other than the status quo and the first choice doesn't have to be huge. Make a choice and take a step. It will be a bit scary because if you are anything like I was you are probably worried about getting it wrong.

But here is the part we all forget: it doesn't matter. If we make a choice and it doesn't turn out the way, we had hoped we can make another choice and see where things go. One thing for certain is that if you don't make choices your situation will never change. No choices mean no action which means no movement. Funnily enough, that is a choice, too. You are choosing not to choose.

We live in a complicated world and that is partly because we make it complicated. If we can go back to remembering we have choices, and that we get to choose ourselves and our lives, life can become simpler. I'm not saying every choice is easy because that's not true. But when we realize we have choices in every aspect of our life then we can truly choose to live.

It takes a courageous heart to be open to choices and to continue to make them and live fully. I don't believe we were born to merely exist. We were born to live our best life. Doing that means making choices. Those choices take us on the adventure of life and can truly take us to some spectacular places if we are willing to choose and go.

Angela's Design Keys for Living Out Loud

Key #15
We all face choices, each and every day. When we step into our life and seize those choices, we embrace our lives and ourselves. The first step is to choose you. From there it is one step at a time towards a magnificent life.

For my personal message
Scan the QR Code with your smart phone
Or go to: https://youtu.be/NRvwDNb3wV8

Chapter Sixteen

Navigating to Be Seen

Navigating to be seen is like navigating a boat. There are a lot of course corrections. With each one, your adventure turns into an ever more amazing journey.
—Angela Wilson

When I was little, I spent many an hour with my Aunt Bea. She was one special lady. I realize now as an adult in my 50s that she was the first person to give me all her attention when we were together. I also realize she was one of the few adults I knew who was always authentic: she did not hide from the world. We had the most wonderful talks, and no subject was off limits—I even remember talking to her about spirits—the supernatural. She would sometimes say that other adults might not be so open minded as she was, and she was correct. I don't ever remember Aunt Bea telling me I couldn't do something. She always made me feel like I could do anything, and she encouraged me to imagine, dream, and use my mind.

Sometimes we would chat as we walked down the road in early summer to pick wild strawberries. She would let me go barefoot as she knew that's what I preferred, although she would have me carry my flip flops or sandals just in case, I needed them. It has been a long time since I've had wild strawberries, but every time I see the little white flowers indicating the berries are on their way, I smile and think of my Aunt Bea.

I also loved picking wild wintergreen with Aunt Bea. It grew on a hill behind her house. These days when I drive past the house where she used to live, I wonder if there is any left on the hill. This past Christmas I saw some wintergreen in a local shop and decided to purchase it, as my husband loves to grow plants. We have an agreement: I buy them, and he takes care of them; tending indoor plants is not one of my superpowers. I gave a little giggle as I felt my Aunt Bea had directed me to that plant. Every time I walk past the plant in my front room now, I think of Aunt Bea, and I smile. She's with me again, in a way. I'm sure she is so proud of what I am doing and that I'm living life and being all of me.

I had snippets of feeling seen as a child and those moments made me feel like maybe I wasn't crazy and maybe I mattered. As a child, it really doesn't take much to feel seen because we haven't yet bought into all the unkind stories floating around us yet and we haven't started creating false stories of our own. It's those stories that hold us in a place of not being seen or feeling like we aren't seen. Oddly enough, as adults, being seen can be one of the scariest but most desirable states in our world. I know it was for me. All I wanted was to be seen. Well, that was what I told myself, but my reality didn't match that desire as I hid, controlled my life, protected myself, and played small. My mental mindset at the time made it impossible for me to be seen because I was so terrified of being judged, of not measuring up. I was doing everything to *not* be seen and at the same time inwardly begging for someone to see me.

Most people only saw the façade I was presenting. That's partially because they were presenting a façade, too. Staying in this hiding state puts conscious and unconscious pressure on us. If we hide long enough, as I did, we forget who we really are and we start believing all the outside opinions about us. We no longer trust our inner knowing. Our heart whisper still tries to get us to listen, but our inner chatter screams so loud it drowns the sound of those whispers out.

Even when we don't think we are being seen there are often people who can see a glimpse of us and have a sense of who we truly are. I realize now that a few people—like my Aunt Bea—did see me at different stages of my life through a lens of "no expectations" and I treasure them for it. Thank goodness they saw me when I couldn't see myself.

Being seen is about interacting in the world as all of me. Full-on me. No apologies. No shifting, morphing, or fitting in. No twisting to please people. No standing back and making others more important, or more comfortable. We all crave to be seen for who we really are. It's a basic human need, want, and desire. But it takes courage to live fully as ourselves, and it takes a willingness to be vulnerable. It also means we are standing strong in our inner knowing and allowing others to stand in theirs. We are thriving and living in the present moment, choosing joy and happiness. You will know when you are being seen because conversations and relationships with like-minded people become more juicy. You can have deep, connected conversations without any fear or doubt creeping in. You feel aligned with your inner wisdom, and you are being authentically you. You feel a sense of inner peace. You no longer feel as if all of you is standing on guard.

When we are seen as a kid, we begin to expect that to be the norm. We *want* people to see us for who we really are. We *want* them to recognize what is in our heart. We *want* them to know us as our authentic selves. Unfortunately, though, for many of us, this is a quest that is not for the weak at heart.

To be seen takes courage. When I became committed to remembering who I am and I decided to embrace life, I was willing to be vulnerable even when it felt like the scariest thing on earth. It took courage to sit in a group of people and openly say "I don't understand," or "that's not me." It took courage to relay my inner thoughts and dreams and not worry about whether people would judge me. When I met my amazing husband, Gord, I was just me. Plain and simple. I joked around and didn't worry about what others thought. I let Gord see the real me from Day One. And I always will.

Allowing people to see you at your heart level is about allowing people to see what I call your "fluffy underbelly" and your vulnerability. Dogs and cats only roll over and let you pet their bellies when they are at ease and can sense you care about them. For a dog to sleep with its belly exposed to you is a sign of their complete trust in you. How many of us are willing to do that? How many of us hide parts of ourselves away because it is easier and less scary? And yet we still crave being seen.

When we don't feel seen we build a story around the idea that we don't matter. We figure we are invisible, and we hide more. The reality is that many people don't see us because they are too busy fighting their own battles.

We have to make some choices in life in order to be seen! But we might get lucky and find people who will see us even when we are hiding ourselves away. In addition to my Aunt Bea. I also had an Aunt Elise and an Uncle Harry in my life who could see me and see my potential. They could also see that I was a futuristic thinker, and I was always striving. Not everyone in my life thought these were good qualities. A former partner used to tell me I wasn't happy with anything. It was tough because I could no more change being a futuristic thinker than change my DNA. It was devastating, and it made me question my sanity. I wondered if there was something wrong with me. I tried to fix myself. The kicker was that there was nothing to fix because I wasn't broken. Thank goodness that period of my life is well in the rearview mirror!

Coming Out to Play

It took courage to step forward on my path and to start letting bits of me shine, to come out and play, and to not retreat at the first sign of judgement. I had a lot of self-doubt while I worked through this period, but it was worth it.

This takes courage. Because now you are opening to let people come inside the armour. Letting people into your inner circle and busting apart the tightly woven blankets is scary, and it is doable. As I mentioned, I used to go over everything I was going to say at least a dozen times before I said it out loud, and now here I am writing a book. And not just any book. A book about my experiences and my journey in hopes that others will find a way to break out of their shadows so much quicker than I did. So, they can truly sense they are not alone in this world.

That is where it all started for me. It was when I realized I wasn't alone, and I didn't have to be alone. Once I started seeing that I could let my guard down a bit, I started to see there were people around me who saw me. The real me! Not the façade I had been showing for so long. What do you think happened as I started letting people in? I didn't believe them when they said kind things about me. I didn't believe in the me they saw because I couldn't. I had to choose to stay and listen. I had to choose to open and receive what was being said instead of just pooh-poohing it and moving on. I was good at negating any compliment or any nice thing that was said about me. In those situations, my inner chatter—my ego—would say, in a somewhat sarcastic tone, "obviously they don't know the real you."

I recently heard a woman say at an event I attended that the ego's job is to protect us. So, when it identifies one bad berry in a bowl of 99 berries it continues to point out the bad berry and will not acknowledge the other 98. The ego is there to save our lives. I had never heard the ego explained that way and it made so much sense.

It made its strong protection tactics seem logical. It also explains why the ego will jump in to protect us when we try to change and open ourselves to being seen. It is why we have to quiet our egoic mind to move forward.

It doesn't mean eliminating it. It means understanding it and coming at things from another angle. Making choices to change our patterns and not live in the past.

Being seen means not living in the past. It means living here and now and expressing yourself. It means living out loud. It means being vulnerable. Some would call this shining your light. We are all here for a reason and once you start realizing that, you start allowing others in. The reason for this in my view is that we start to become comfortable in our own skin. We discover how to love ourselves. And we stop looking outside of ourselves for all the answers…and for happiness. From that space we are stepping up to be seen. We are letting our light shine.

I've had to change my habit of negating the qualities people recognize in me that make me who I am. You know—the unique qualities that make me Angela. For example, my openness to listen, my courageous heart, my willingness to keep taking steps even when I'm not sure what the steps are, and my ability to believe in the future and what can be accomplished. The key to doing this is to find a community of people who are loving and genuine at heart. You'll know them when you find them. When I did, it felt like I was home. I felt like I could be me. The beauty was that I *could* be. In that environment, I started opening up and sharing my thoughts and feelings. I felt safe. It created an arena for me to start tearing down my protective layers and to start quieting my inner chatter. Piece by piece, the art of being seen fell into place.

It was a bit scary at times as I had become quite comfortable in my tightly woven blankets of protection but as I released them, I began to feel free. The energy I gained back was amazing. I was no longer using my energy to slog through the day. Instead, I was using it to be me and jump into things I'm passionate about. It opened me to a world of dreaming and planning for my future. I was finally excited about my future because for the first time I felt I had a hand in it. When I was hiding, everything I did was focused on keeping those blankets tightly woven and intertwined so I could protect myself… and I did no dreaming. Life was all about getting through each day, one at a time. I did no planning for the future because I couldn't see past the moment in which I found myself. On top of that, I learned not to talk about the future because I didn't want to appear ungrateful or unhappy.

Choosing to Be Seen

Can you see how freeing it is for your soul and your heart when you make the choice to be seen? Can you see how the stress and pressure releases from you? Can you see how life can become amazing and magical? It may be hard to see at this moment to the full extent of what is possible for you, but I'm guessing you can see glimmers of it. I bet you have a few special people in your life who see you, and with whom you feel at peace. These are the people you don't hide from or, if you do, it's only to a small extent. Allow yourself this gift. It is a gift that lives inside you. You were born with it. Tap into it. Feel it. It boils down to you being you and shining that out to the world.

Each time you take a step toward that your heart will open more. For me, as this was happening, I started to see more beauty around me. I noticed all the beauty that Mother Nature offers me each day. As part of my journey, I started a daily practice of reminding myself of all I have to be grateful for. Gratitude goes a long way towards being seen in the world and it opens your heart to receive even more.

You will definitely go through phases where you can't relate to people you have known for years. Some of these people may exit from your life. Unfortunately, that is one of the hard lessons I had to learn. I didn't comprehend that not everyone was supposed to remain in my life. Sometimes even the people we thought would be there forever might leave because our relationships become less congruent as we open. Here is something I can tell you from experience: as painful as that may feel when it is happening, other people will come into your life. Maybe not immediately, but they will come, and they will see you shining. Because they can see you. I've learned that everyone comes into our life for at least a season. Some stay for a couple of seasons and some stay for a lifetime of seasons. Some may drift out for a couple of seasons and then come back in, and your friendship will be even stronger. This is because you are in a different spot in your life, and they can enter back in as now the relationship can flourish. They all touch our lives in different ways, and they all add something to our journey.

If we don't allow ourselves to be seen so we can keep certain people in our life, then we are robbing ourselves of living our best life. Because we are not being true to ourselves. I miss some of the people who are no longer in my life, and I can clearly see why some of them needed to leave. I know for certain now that I wouldn't change a thing if it meant I had to go back to not being seen.

When I opened my heart and allowed people in, my life truly began, and I truly started living. I deserve to live my life out loud being 100% Angela 100% of the time. You deserve that, too. Close your eyes for a moment and imagine how that feels. Allow yourself to feel how freeing it is to be you in all your glory.

As an exercise to cement this in a little more deeply try looking in the mirror each morning while you are brushing your teeth and appreciate the person staring back at you. Take her all in. This moves you toward more self-love as you appreciate you. More self-love gives you more confidence to live your life out loud because when you are not being 100% of you, you will feel it and you'll want to move back toward being you. Next, as you go through your day, be aware of the moments when you feel totally centred so you can come back to that feeling when/if you shift off of it. Finally, as you go through your day use your voice and courageously share your thoughts. It will be hard at first but keep taking steps toward it. Remember: each step makes the next one easier.

As you go on your journey to being seen I hope that when you doubt if it is worth it, you come back to the feeling you just had when you stopped for a moment and imagined it. That feeling is always there to tap into, and it can be a great tool to use whenever you need it. The other tool is to find people you know see you, and when you doubt yourself, have a conversation with them so you can remember and shift the doubt. It is a process, but one that is well worth taking the time to pursue.

Remember the key I mentioned: you are never alone. Once you take this to heart, believe in yourself, and love yourself in all your magnificence, then being seen becomes a way of life. It is no longer scary. One of the greatest gifts you can allow yourself is to be seen and to love yourself.

Angela's Design Keys to Living Out Loud

Key #16
Choosing to be seen and allowing yourself to be seen takes courage. If you want to live a magical life and be you, you will need to tap into that courage. The joy of not hiding and being all of you is magnificent and ultimately rewarding. There is only one you: stand up and allow people to see you.

For my personal message
Scan the QR Code with your smart phone
Or go to: https://youtu.be/PICtEc77ePY

Chapter Seventeen

Life as a Double Agent

> *When you can release the double life you are living your life becomes freer, more fulfilling, and more magical. It's time to embrace the magic and live fully as you…no more living a double life.*
> —Angela Wilson

In my early days of learning how to play golf, another couple joined my then-partner and me. The wife had never golfed before. I thought, "*finally, someone that I can relate to out on the course!*" Well, that didn't turn out the way I expected, as she whooped my butt. My partner explained to me that *of course* she was better than I was because she was a natural athlete, and I was not.

Can you imagine where my mind went from there? To a very dark spot. It was quite a while before I golfed again and when I did, I constantly reminded myself that of course I wasn't any good, nor would I be, because I was not athletic. When we have these stories playing in the back of our minds everything is filtered through them and when we evolve into a truer version of ourselves we realize they have no basis in reality.

Golf is now a game I love. I'm not particularly good at it but I've made peace with that idea. For me now, it is all about being outside in the sunshine and having fun. At one point I was a very avid golfer and golfed as many as four times per week. I was a member of the club at my favourite course, and I golfed with the same group of people most of the time. It was lots of fun, but at one point I found I became tense whenever I came to an area of the course that had been a challenge for me. I began to expect a challenge, and this would dampen my spirits as I got close.

Golf can be a fickle game because even the best golfer has a bad day. It became a battle between me and the course. Then my wonderful husband suggested we go out to a different course, not keep score, and just have fun. It was a turning point: I realized I could just relax and have fun. I also learned that if others didn't want to golf with me because I didn't meet their expectations, well, that was just too bad. I learned to enjoy the game again and still do because I let my expectations subside.

Have you ever placed expectations on yourself that were totally unrealistic? It's even harder if you are a perfectionist. Not only are you beating yourself up and trying to control everything, but you are also bending, twisting, and morphing from all angles to live up to what you think others expect of you, and what you have decided you should expect of yourself. Those two sets of expectations are very different. They are impossible to meet, and they put you in a further state of self-doubt and feeling worth-less. I'm even going to say possibly even a state of self-loathing because that is what it was for me. A lot of the time I didn't like myself very much. This dislike came from my inner chatter about how I didn't measure up, which kicked off another vicious circle.

When you place expectations on yourself you are trying to squish yourself into an identity that doesn't fit. You are setting yourself up for failure, instead of success. I admit expectations can motivate us to strive to do better. But for me, they were always a weapon. They were unrealistic.

There's a difference between *expecting* yourself to be the best version of yourself that you can be and *wanting* to be the best version of yourself that you can be. My view is that the first sentence sets a hard and fast ultimatum while the second one allows us to be ourselves, to grow, and to learn. Which would you rather use to guide your life? When we are living in the land of expectations, we are always chasing something, like the donkey chasing the carrot at the end of the stick that he can never reach. It wears us down and turns life into a slogfest instead of a joyful experience.

When I was living in the land of impossible expectations, I felt like I was trapped under my protective layers and yet I wanted to portray to the rest of the world that all was okay. Over time it became increasingly difficult to keep up the façade and I felt like some sort of "double agent." I couldn't let the truth of either side be exposed. If I did, catastrophic things might happen. At least that's the way it felt to me.

And so, I was extremely hard on myself. I used to say that no one else needed to point out my failings because I was already on it. It became an automatic response. If I put myself down and beat myself up, it was harder for anyone else to do it. It took the sting out of it. It shredded my self-esteem to the point of almost zero. This was a horrible way to live! Even now I have to be very aware to keep from slipping back into that way of being. I have to be conscious to not apologize for myself out of habit as I used to live with the assumption that I was wrong and everyone else was right. In addition, I felt that surely if something were amiss it had to be my fault.

When I look back now, I can't find an area in my life where I wasn't hard on myself. I didn't think I was smart enough. Which led to superhuman efforts to make sure I had everything just "so." When I did make a mistake, I said horrible things to myself. I would have never spoken to anyone else that way. I remember making a decent-sized mistake at work. When I talked to the person I worked for I fully anticipated they would fire me. I was in a massive state of stress. I apologized, explained how the mistake had happened, what

I was going to do to fix it, and the process I was going to put in place so it couldn't happen again. I waited to hear how incompetent I was, and that my contract was ended. It didn't happen. Instead, my employer said, "What is going on, this is not like you…are you okay? Of course, the real answer was, "no," which they already knew. The relationship I mentioned earlier had recently ended and I was trying to hold myself together. Most days it was a battle-and-a-half.

It turned out the big story I had conjured prior to the meeting was nothing even close to the reality. Can you guess what I did next? Well, I started beating myself up for being such a fool. It was a vicious circle and one I'm glad to be finished with. The stress of carrying around a massive amount of self-doubt was a factor in adrenal fatigue down the line. As I mentioned earlier, adrenal fatigue occurs when your adrenals are overworked from releasing large amounts of cortisol to combat stress levels in your body. The adrenals can't produce enough cortisol to meet the demand. We can recover from this, but we must choose to stop allowing excessive stress into our life. We must choose to be kind to ourselves. We must choose to treat ourselves the way we treat others. We must choose to love ourselves.

When we are keeping up a façade, we get into a mode of control. Everything becomes about control. The deeper we get into it, the more control we need to have. We don't want to show any chinks in the armour. We want to have the best-looking façade we can in hope we can remain hidden. We don't want people questioning anything! It took courage for me to shift away from that way of being and I can't even imagine living like that now.

Learning That I Mattered

With mentoring and practice I learned to lean in and understand that I mattered. As I started to realize how horribly I had talked to myself for years I chose to stop. I would consciously look in the mirror and when the old conversation would start up, I would stop it and say "No, not today." I also learned the art of not engaging my inner chatter. When it wanted to go on a rant, I would observe it and not buy into what it was saying. That took a lot of practice, but I made it. I would also consciously "turn the volume down" when my inner chatter would start its blah-blah-blahing. Or, if you're old enough to remember the Peanuts cartoon, I would make the chatter sound like Charlie Brown's teacher.

I believe the key to it all for me was talking to people and letting them know what I was thinking and feeling. Boy, that took a lot of courage! But if I was going to stop being a double agent and live my life as the best version of me, it was the only choice to make.

The exercise here I invite you to try is what I just described. When your inner chatter is ramping up make a conscious break. Something like, No, not today," or, "Not Happening," works well. The idea is to come up with the right words for you to cut it off sharply. When you do this make sure not to dwell on the story you were about to tell yourself. You have evidence from your life that what your inner chatter was trying to say is not true. Think of the wonderful things you have done and how far you have come on your journey. Make sure if it is persisting to turn the volume down on it or change the voice to something that makes you laugh. It's a great way to interrupt it. Once you interrupt it enough you can start keeping it at bay.

A side effect of trying to control everything was that I could appear to be somewhat stand-offish to others. That is far from the truth of how I really felt, but I heard it repeatedly. The reality was that I was uncomfortable in my skin and terrified that anyone would find out. Seriously, what would people think? That's it in a nutshell. I was so wrapped up in what others would think that I wasn't thinking for myself. I was going down every rabbit hole I thought others expected of me. What I have come to learn, through my journey of remembering Angela, is that the only opinion about me that matters is mine. I'm the one who needs to be peaceful within me. The old saying "you can't make everyone happy" comes to mind. You are the important one. Make *you* happy! Happiness comes from within, and you find it when you stop beating yourself up and trying to control everything. You find it when you start living a life where joy and happiness are your overarching choice points. It's how I live my life today. It's what allows me to continue to grow, learn, and move forward in the world.

A subsection of beating yourself up and controlling everything, as I alluded to earlier in this chapter, is perfectionism. In my case, it seemed to arise as a reaction to people criticizing and teasing me and telling me I wasn't good at things. I had a kind of an "I'll show you" response. As I got older it became a learned habit and it took over. I expected myself to be prefect at everything I tried or set out to do right from the get-go. I didn't give myself any leeway. Funny…I gave plenty to everyone else.

The perfectionism played perfectly into the hand of my ritual of beating myself up. None of us is prefect. We can't be: we are human. And yet I expected this of myself. I demanded it of myself. So, when it inevitably didn't happen, I would jump to my go-to move of flinging harsh nasty words through my head. Then I would demand perfection from myself again in the next circumstance. What do you think happened? What it felt like was an endless loop. I set myself up with a lot of ammunition…it was spectacular. If this vicious circle were an Olympic event, I could have been a gold medalist. Of course, it never would make it to the Olympics, as it is way too cruel. Have you experienced anything similar?

Once I started to shift my stories and change my mindset, my world opened. It is rare now to have my inner chatter run the show and beat me up. I'm fortunate to have had many people in my corner be patient with me. To love me. To support me. Some people had to walk out of my life as their season with me had ended. I've been able to bring my health back so I'm no longer in adrenal fatigue and I'm making more leaps and bounds in that area as my life opens more and more.

As all the old fades away into the past I continue to focus more on what my dreams are for the future. I let joy, happiness, and dreams fill my life. I let the old slights, stories, and protections slide away. It's a much freer way to live. It's a more peaceful way to live. It's a healthier way to live. It allows me to live as me. Ah…what a relief! It's available to you, too.

Angela's Design Keys to Living Out Loud

Key #17
Strive to be the best version of you every day. Let the double agent life and the expectations that go along with it slide out of your life. Allow yourself to live freer and breathe.

For my personal message
Scan the QR Code with your smart phone
Or go to: https://youtu.be/U3z8PCjVVZ8

Chapter Eighteen

Being Alone

*When you decide to love yourself you are never
alone, and when you have time on your own
from that perspective you, will be in a magical space.*
— Angela Wilson

When I was a young girl I went to Brownies, then Girl Guides, and then Pathfinders. At each level, I strove to be a part of the group, and to earn as many badges as I could. I was setting myself up for failure as I expected myself to be able to accomplish everything the other girls did and, of course, that didn't happen.

One reason was that my skill set was not the same because I was uniquely me. But I didn't understand that. Instead, I would beat myself up for not being good enough. I also expected myself to be popular enough to get the other girls to vote me in as patrol leader. I did eventually make it to patrol leader but there were a lot of hurts inside before it happened. And, finally, as I've mentioned before, I was desperate to be liked: little girls can smell that and feed off it. Other girls teased me for being too big, for not having the "in" shoes, for my haircut, and for what felt like anything else they could dream up. Sometimes I had a lot of fun but at the same time I got a lot of lessons around not fitting in, not being well-liked, and not mattering.

You may be wondering why I didn't just try something else. As a little girl I grew up in a rural area and options were limited. Those three groups were held locally in our town which meant I could walk there from my house. The organizations themselves are wonderful. As an adult, I went back to Girl Guides as a leader. I wanted to help young girls navigate through their early teenage years more easily than I did. I hadn't thought of becoming a Guide Leader before a friend suggested it. My first response was, "but I'm not a mom so how would I become a leader?"

You see, when I was a girl, the leaders were always moms and that notion stuck with me. I have to say I had a lot of fun times with the girls when we were doing activities, going camping, and singing. I felt like I was making a difference. Then the old dreads started coming up as politics got in the way and I started trying to prove myself again. I began trying to meet everyone's expectations and I was making myself miserable. When it got to the point where I would come home in tears and started feeling anxious about even going to the meetings, I decided it was time to find something else.

Being alone was one of my biggest fears and I took a lot of action over the years to avoid it. I was terrified that no one would love me and that I would spend the remainder of my life on my own. This was a biproduct of not feeling worthy and desperately wanting to fit in. If I could just get people to like me enough, then I would be surrounded by friends and my life would be full. I would finally feel worthy. I was relying on others for my worthiness and my happiness, instead of relying on myself.

Honestly, this piece is probably one of the hardest areas I've had to shift on my journey. I had tied my value to other people's opinions of me. I made everyone else more important than me. This plagued my decisions and drove my lack of decisions. I didn't want to make anyone upset or angry. The fear running inside me said that if I did, they would leave. Cut and dry, no room for anything else. It was a horrible way to live. However, it correlated with the emptiness I felt inside.

The end of my relationship confirmed for me that I was unlovable. I wasn't good enough for my partner to love so he left, and I was alone. Maybe you have heard the saying, "there is your view, the other person's view, and then the truth." You can apply it to many aspects of your life. I thought I was unlovable but that wasn't the truth.

When I was confronted with such blatant evidence of how flawed my thinking had been I had two choices…to stay in the spot that I was in or to make the choice to change. Thank God I chose to change because it did transform my life into a glorious adventure. To be honest it didn't feel like I had a choice at first. It was all I could do to breathe and get through each day. It wasn't a short journey or an easy one but with each step I knew there was more available to me. Thank goodness I had people around me to love and support me when I could only muster breathing. I began to realize how small I had been playing. I started to sense and feel how incongruent that was with who I was at my heart.

Who I was at my heart…let's start there. When you feel invisible for as long as I did you get to a point where you assume you actually *are* invisible, and you don't question it anymore. The first step I took was to surround myself with friends I felt I could trust. Trust is important. I didn't trust myself initially and I made some missteps. I started remembering who I was, who I really was on the inside—who I was in my heart. When we don't remember who we are we no longer trust our inner knowing—our intuition—and we don't allow it to guide us.

Eventually I learned to listen to my inner knowing again. And bit by bit I started trusting myself again. Do you know what happens when you have that back in your life? Well, now your "bullshit" metre is back online. The missteps of trusting the wrong people rarely happen anymore because your inner knowing gives you the nudge that something isn't right, and you listen to it. When I got to this stage, I felt like I was me again...like an old friend had come home.

Once I remembered who I was, and many of my fears had subsided, now came the work of self-love. It was a harder journey than remembering who I was because I was so well practiced at tearing myself down. I also had to start seeing the evidence in my life that showed me it was okay to love myself.

By the time I had learned to love myself I no longer feared being alone. I accepted that being on my own was okay and I could even enjoy it. I stopped looking for the evidence that I was unlovable, unworthy, and didn't fit in. Instead, I started treating myself the way I treated others who were near and dear to me. It is amazing: when you take this approach, life becomes joyful, full, and adventurous. I now love my life. The key was learning to love myself. I now stop myself when negative inner chatter might try to creep in. I remind myself I am unique and special, and I don't deserve to get dragged down any of the rabbit holes my old patterns might want to take me down. It is my choice and I choose to feel good and to love myself. It also means I'm okay spending time with me. If I ever start to feel blue and doubt myself, I look for evidence of how far I have come since my dark yesteryears. I no longer compare myself to others. Instead, I compare myself to who I used to be. When you do that it's hard not to smile and love yourself. I learned this technique from Laura Gisborne, a beautiful soul, and a wise mentor.

I would invite you to spend time with yourself. Start by blocking off even a half hour once per week. Curl up with a yummy cup of tea and a good book or journal. Spend part of the time in stillness if you can. You might have to build to stillness but try it even for a minute or two at first. Light a nice candle and create a tranquil atmosphere. This is "you" time; make it sacred. If you are more of an outdoors person, take that time to go for a walk by yourself. Take in all the sights, smells, and sounds of nature. Hug a tree and feel the bark against your skin. The important thing is to be you and be by yourself. Once this feels comfortable increase to a couple of times a week and go from there. You've got this!

Finding the Love of My Life

The other part of this glorious adventure? I found the love of my life. I give thanks every day that he is in my life. More than nine years from the day we met we still talk for hours, and I have never once felt judged by him. He is always of love and assistance because he knows I want to be the best version of myself. He encourages me to go after my dreams. Actually, he is the one who really got me back to dreaming. My dreams for my life are what pull me forward. These dreams are intertwined with our love because I love spending time with my husband. He is my biggest champion, and I am so grateful for his love and support in all I do. There was a time in my life when I never would have believed a relationship like this was out there waiting for me. Miracles do happen.

Being yourself fully in every minute, of every day, and standing firmly in your life means that you are never alone. You always have you, and you always fit in. If you have to change yourself even a tiny bit from who you truly are then you are not supposed to fit in with that group, person, or relationship. We are meant to be fully ourselves all the time and to allow our uniqueness to soar in the world. We are not meant to be small in any sense of the word because to do that means we have changed ourselves to meet some expectation, perceived or real. Being afraid to be alone made me change who I was on so many fronts. And because of those changes I couldn't possibly get to where my brain wanted me to go. Once I learned to love myself and remember who I was I could finally start living my life. Start living the journey. Be on the glorious adventure. You deserve to love yourself and you deserve to be all of you.

Angela's Design Keys to Living Out Loud

Key #18
Loving yourself is the best gift you can give yourself. It opens you to living as the best version of yourself and it opens you into the life you deserve. The journey to loving yourself is a courageous one. When you choose that journey the adventure you ignite will be amazing!

For my personal message
Scan the QR Code with your smart phone
Or go to: https://youtu.be/20JKGWTYyg0

Chapter Nineteen

Being the Authentic You

*The greatest gift you can give yourself is to allow
your authentic self to shine out into the world.
This powerful gift opens you up to possibilities, dreams,
adventure, and magic.*
—Angela Wilson

Have you ever done something that you knew felt wrong, but you did it anyway? An example from my university days was when I dated a guy I knew was a total mismatch for me. But I was caught up in the idea that someone liked me, rather than listening to my inner knowing, which was telling me he was not trustworthy. I was going against my inner knowing. When that happens it doesn't feel very good, does it? When you stay in that place for too long, you lose yourself. You can stay in the holding pattern of misalignment for years. I have to say, though, that if I had been more conscious of my thoughts and actions, I would have understood I could choose differently.

Here's an example of what it looks like to follow your inner knowing. My husband and I were travelling in Greece. We were meandering through Athens and walked through a wonderful area where all kinds of restaurants had set tables up in the street. We love walking through areas like that, with all the delicious-smelling food, the wonderful conversations, and laughter buzzing around us, and the amazing colours that treat our eyes. As we were talking, we realized there were fewer and fewer of these street-side restaurants around us, and the area had changed. Almost on a dime we both stopped walking, turned, looked at each other, and said "we shouldn't be here." Both of us at the same time had an uneasy feeling and our inner knowing told us to get out of the area into which we had strayed. And so, we did. We listened to our inner voices.

By contrast, earlier in my life I wouldn't listen to those uneasy feelings. Instead, I just kept morphing myself into whatever version of Angela I thought other people wanted me to be. I can think of a couple of different trips when I was uncomfortable with a situation, but I never spoke up because I didn't want to make any waves. Meanwhile, inside I was crawling out of my skin. I was not being authentically Angela. I was being the friend I thought people wanted me to be. I was being the daughter and sister I thought others wanted me to be. I was being the partner I thought my partner wanted me to be. I was being the accountant I thought others wanted me to be. What I wasn't being, was Angela.

When I finally got out of my own way, I started to listen to my inner knowing and began to trust that voice. My experience has shown that voice will never lead me astray. The key is, though, that I have to listen. If you let your inner chatter weigh in and mess with the message your inner knowing is trying to share, you will let yourself down.

This whole book has been building to this very point: to the discussion of being the authentic you. Are you asking yourself what that means? We've already touched on parts of it.

What I mean by the authentic you, is the you at your heart base. The unwavering you. The you who shows up regardless of the circumstances or the people around you. The sparkly little three-year-old you. If you get present to your thoughts, you can come up with at least a vision of her. You remember she used to laugh, and dance, and play. Most of all she shone her light and was completely *her*. No limits. No morphing. No pleasing. One hundred percent her all the time…living with unlimited possibilities swirling around her. This is how we are meant to live. It isn't an illusion or a dream. It isn't a "nice-to-be-someday."

You have read how I limited myself from an early age until a few years ago when I knew things had to change. I mentioned my breaking point came with the end of a relationship. Honestly, I had no clue who I was when that happened. I felt like the rug of life had been pulled out from under my feet and I had landed on my ass so hard I might never get up. Inside me, however, there was a voice. It started as a whisper I didn't recognize at all. That whisper was my heart voice. It comes to everyone in different forms. For me it is a voice that whispers through at the base of my throat and the top of my chest. If you place your left hand so your thumb and middle finger are touching your collar bone, you feel the exact spot. I pay attention to that whisper, as it guides me. The voice that goes through my head is different. It is the one I have described as my inner chatter, and it tries to rationalize everything.

You may be thinking this sounds a bit "out there," but it really isn't. It isn't even any kind of "woo." We each have an inner knowing. It is your instinct guiding you. It has been guiding you all along, you just might have forgotten how to listen to it or hear it. When that happens, you are misaligned with your true self. Your inner chatter and the rest of the world are running the show.

Choosing to Move Forward

Getting out of my own way involved a choice to make a change. It meant allowing myself to open up and stop putting up roadblocks at every turn. It was about disregarding the way things had been and making a choice to move forward. To move forward I had to go through the process of unraveling my protective layers. I had to quiet my inner chatter. I had to start listening to my inner knowing. I had to realize happiness comes from within. And I had to accept that being me is pretty spectacular.

The personal development work I did let a ray of sunlight penetrate my protective layers. It assisted me to start in a small way to listen to my heart voice. I learned that maybe there was another way to view who I was. I also learned that maybe the whisper I had heard over the years that had told me there was more to me than was meeting the eye *wasn't so crazy after all*. I'm so grateful I took the step to take that first personal development class that showed up in my life. Oh, in those early stages I had many doubts and I questioned everything. And I kept taking steps.

As I started to listen to my inner knowing through my heart voice, I had to learn how to trust it again. Was I really hearing it or was I making it all up? I questioned that a lot, in the beginning. I had been so deep in the well of not mattering and thinking everyone else was so much more advanced than I was, that when I heard someone else talk about how their inner knowing came to them, I would play the comparison game.

Someone else's inner knowing always seemed more real, grander, and more special. I remember getting together with an amazing group of women on a retreat. At the start of it some were discussing how their guidance spoke to them through images they would get, or words which were communicated to them. My answer was always, "I don't get it. I don't hear or see things. I have no idea what you are talking about." That response came from my inner chatter, my egoic brain, that had for so long told me I didn't measure up. So, naturally it was still trying to tell me exactly that. This was also another way for me to make everyone else more important.

I couldn't possibly have inner knowing like others because I wasn't as deserving. It took me some time to realize my guidance comes through, as I mentioned, with a whispered feeling, and it is all good because we are each unique and how we hear our guidance is as well.

You might be wondering at this moment if it is worth it? Should I bother to try to bust out of my cocoon? I can only speak from my experience and from that place the answer is "YES!" When I started to listen to my heart voice again, my life changed. It continues to change as my knowing grows deeper and deeper and I trust it more and more. Once I let that go and started really owning the fact that I do matter, life changed.

The final exercise I would invite you to try is to get quiet and listen. I know that probably sounds funny. What I mean is breathe deeply and quiet your mind. Quiet the logical inner chatter brain and listen. Do you sense another voice or a feeling? Be open and just stay in quietness. Your heart voice will reach out to you. When you notice how it does, say thank you and acknowledge you heard it. This can take a bit of time if you haven't been listening for a while. It's okay. Try this every day for two weeks, then expand it to three weeks, and eventually you will just hear it, feel it, and you'll be back in touch with your heart voice.

Deserving a Wonderful Life

Bit by bit, life became easier, brighter, joyful, more peaceful, freer. I started to live my life with real purpose, and I began embracing the idea that I deserved to have a wonderful life. My husband and I have an amazing time together and each day feels like a gift to me. I've expanded my work to be more creative and to be of assistance to other women who find themselves limited in ways similar to what I experienced; I am committed to helping them see that life can be full of unlimited possibilities like mine is. My business, Angela Unlimited, is built around exactly that mission (www.angelaunlimited.com).

It took a while for my business to come to fruition, but it did. I first had to realign with my essence and trust my inner knowing. The more I listened to my guidance, and the less I listened to my inner chatter, the more I started to realize I could trust myself and trust my inner knowing. I learned that when I listen to myself and don't get caught up in the drama of life, I can see possibilities around me. It required me to take time to marvel at the beauty around me every day and be grateful for it. As I listened more to my inner knowing I got a strong sense of the differences between it and my inner chatter. I began trusting the feelings as real. If I hadn't, I would never have taken the chance to create a business: my inner chatter would have told me it was not possible because I wasn't smart enough or talented enough. Neither are true. Both are just old stories I had learned which led to me limiting myself.

It's interesting that the first seed of Angela Unlimited came shortly after that previous relationship ended as I sat in the parking lot of a Starbucks restaurant crying because at the time my world was so messed up, I didn't think I could afford a latte. I had bought one latte a week prior to the end of the relationship and now I couldn't see how I could afford it. I remember crying and thinking, *"this can't be true. How do others get through this? How do others manage?"*

I had my own accounting practice and made a decent living but there never seemed to be enough and now that it was just me, on my own, I didn't see how I would make it work. All I could do was breathe and put one foot in front of the other. It was at that moment the seed for Angela Unlimited was born as I knew in my heart that one day, I wanted to be able to assist other women, so they didn't have to land in the same pit of misery I had found myself.

I completely set aside the idea of Angela Unlimited for a while as my task at hand was to remember me. When you are congruent with who you authentically are, things come back around. Six years after my Parking Lot Moment my business ideas started to coalesce. My personal life was blissfully happy as my soul mate (now my husband) was by my side. I was still learning about me and honestly, I still am because that topic is about a journey, not a single destination we are trying to "get to."

Over a glass of wine in Spain I told my husband my idea. I said, "I don't know where this is going but I know in my heart,"—can you say heart voice talking?—"it is something I want to do." Well, a few years later...here I am the Founder and Chief Unlimited Officer of Angela Unlimited!

I'm explaining this to you because I want you to see that when you make the choice to come back to being your authentic self, you can go after your dreams. You believe you can do it, and you believe you deserve it. You no longer hide in the shadow of self-doubt and make yourself small. As I've mentioned, this takes time, choice, and a willingness to be you. We hold inside us such immense courage and it's always available to us. We just don't always recognize it and our inner chatter tells us it doesn't exist. When you step into alignment with your authentic self you can sense your courage. You just need to believe in you. You need to trust you!

I now live in joy and happiness most of the time. I'm not afraid of getting something wrong and I'm not afraid of the judgements of others. I stopped letting that fear run my life. Wouldn't you rather be happy than give in to your fear of what others think? Do you think you can live aligned with the authentic you and yet still be afraid of what others think? You really can't because then you are giving your power away to them and your alignment goes out the window. Again, we will at times get things wrong because we are human and we're on a journey of growth and expansion. I've found the journey is richer when we listen to our heart voice, stay centred in our essence, and trust our inner knowing. From that place life becomes full of unlimited possibilities.

I now look for the possibilities around me instead of thinking there are none. This has led me to living my life with more awareness because awareness is key. Once you are aware of where you are you can make a choice to change your circumstances. That is, what I did when I took my six- year journey. I had to get clear on where I was and what was going on.

With that knowledge, I could go in a different direction than I had in the past. But until I understood that, I couldn't make the choice to change how I was living, as I couldn't see the pitfalls I was stepping into daily. Without awareness, we just bump along and let our fears rule us. When you are looking for the possibilities in life instead of just surviving you are coming from a place of abundance. My life now feels full and meaningful. I live in gratitude every day for all the wonderful things in my life. I've chosen to allow my creativity out into the world. I'm focused on the beauty around me, and I'm focused on my dreams. I found that once I started being grateful for aspects of my life, my focus on "surviving" decreased, and my ability to thrive grew.

It's important to remember that possibilities come with dreams and it's important to know what it is you want to create. You don't need to know how to get there you just need to know where you want to go. You get clear on what you want and then start taking action based on the possibilities that show up. That's your job. Knowing what possibilities will show up and how to leverage them are not.

You might be thinking that sounds too simple. It is simple. We just make it difficult because we have been told—and so we learned—things are supposed to be hard. What if you chose to no longer buy into the old story that life is supposed to be hard? When I let that old story slide off into the sunset things changed drastically and I could write a new story. One where I got to create my life. My dreams may not look exactly like I have them pictured at the moment and that's okay by me because what I've learned is they will inevitably be even better than I could have imagined and align with me even more. A great example of this was when I wanted to see the Serengeti and the animals roaming free. I didn't narrow the dream down to specify

"Tanzania" or that I would go with the camera club. It showed up perfectly and it was an experience of a lifetime that gave me amazing memories. I have a new dream with regards to the Serengeti and that is to return with my husband and some close friends. I can only dream with what I know today, the amount of imagination I have available to me right now. I always tack onto the end of my dream…"or that which I can't even imagine yet." This opens me to more abundance and more possibilities. That is what I want for you, too.

Now, be aware as you are going through this journey that you will have nay-sayers. My advice is to ignore them, the best you can. They will try to convince you that this is all too hard, you are too fragile, or you don't have what it takes. I give you full permission to stand tall and say, "YES, I DO!" You have the strength and courage to change your life and start living life unlimited. You can play full in and design your life to be whatever your heart desires. Let your heart sing to you and to the world. We are here right now—why not make this the most spectacular life ever? The beauty of it is, it doesn't matter what has happened up until this point. All of that is in the past. The key is right here, right now. Not yesterday, not a month ago, not a year ago. Right now. Deal only with what is in the present moment because you can't change what happened even a moment ago because it's over.

Start dreaming and creating the life you want to live. Make the choice to live an unlimited life and experience it to the fullest. You have the courage inside of you. I believe in you. It's time for you to believe in you! It's time to live your best unlimited life!

Angela's Design Keys to Living Out Loud

Key #19
Tapping into your courage and living as your authentic self is a magnificent way to live. It's time! Be you! Shine all of you out into the world!

For my personal message
Scan the QR Code with your smart phone
Or go to: https://youtu.be/VWQHSfuFQxQ

Bibliography

Elizabeth Gilbert, Big Magic, Creative Living Beyond Fear, Riverhead Books, An imprint of Penguin Random House LLC, New York, 2015, page 258.

Theodore Roosevelt speech "Citizenship in a Republic" given at the Sobonne in Paris on April 23, 1910

Brown, Brené, *I Thought It Was Just Me (But it Wasn't)*, Avery, New York, pg 127.

About the Author

Angela Wilson is a Designated Accountant, as well as an author, speaker, coach and mentor, for women. She is the Founder and Chief Unlimited Office of Angela Unlimited. She created Angela Unlimited to assist women to transform the mindsets that are limiting them from living the life they deserve but are not yet living. The passion to help women comes from Angela's own experience, starting out as a child with unlimited possibilities in life, to having limits put on her. After going through very dark times where she questioned who she really was, and asking, "Isn't there more to life than this?"

After deciding that she would no longer live life small, and quiet, she decided it was time to go out and grab the life she was here to live - a life of unlimited possibilities.

Her journey took courage and strength, and she knows other women have it in them to do the same thing, they just need someone to show them they are not alone, and that there is a life of Unlimited Possibilities ahead of them. Angela is here to do just that with her book, Living Out Loud – Design Your Life of Unlimited Possibilities.

www.ingramcontent.com/pod-product-compliance
Lightning Source LLC
Chambersburg PA
CBHW050251010526
44107CB00003B/279